The author may be contacted at:

http://faithexperience.blog

Legend of scripture references used:

NASB	New American Standard Bible
NKJV	New King James
NIV	New International Bible
NASB	New American Standard Bible
NLT	New Living Translation.
KJV	King James Version
ERV	Easy to Read Bible
NCV	New Century Version
NET	New English Translation
CSB	Christian Standard Bible
AMP	Amplified Bible
MESSAGE	Message Bible

Introduction to Living in Grace

Series 1

The following pages contain three months of daily readings covering five days a week Monday to Friday. Each day is numbered in order to help you keep track of your progress. Drawn from many years in the Christian ministry with my wife Jennifer these pages contain true experiences and insights gained in Pastoral life. Some topics cover a few days and take the form of a simple Bible study, others just one or two days, but all with a practical message for your day to day walk as a believer. Each one takes just a few minutes but gives you something to ponder on throughout the day if you so wish. My prayer is that these pages will encourage, bless and strengthen you in your walk with the Lord whether you are a new or mature believer.

Please remember though as you turn these pages that God's Grace although highlighted here at no point ever supersedes or overshadows His other Glorious attributes, to do so leads to error and spiritual deception. Good Theology teaches us that all God's wonderful qualities must be kept in balance.

I want to add personal thanks to Jennifer for her help and patience with me as I have written this book, Bev Taylor for her proof reading and kind words, Ian Spencer for his commendation and Ben Ryan for help in the book cover design.

Copies are available from the author personally, via Amazon Books online or my blog on https://faithexperience.com

Adopted by Jesus!

Over the next few days we will look at our glorious adoption, take time to ponder and pray that God will give you a greater understanding of this amazing truth.

> *For you did not receive the spirit of bondage again to fear, but you received the Spirit of adoption by whom we cry out, "Abba, Father."16 The Spirit Himself bears witness with our spirit that we are children of God, 17 and if children, then heirs; heirs of God and joint heirs with Christ, if indeed we suffer with Him, that we may also be glorified together.*
> Romans 8: 15 (NIV)

This passage deals with the subject of spiritual adoption. Often something we know about but perhaps don't always fully grasp. A good definition of adoption is this, "all those that come to Jesus are admitted into God's eternal family and He guarantees to keep them in and for His Son Jesus Christ"

Often our text in Romans is just interpreted in a way that implies we don't have to entertain general fear in our lives, so it's important to understand the context Paul is talking in.

Our passage today tells us a number of things about what it really means to be adopted into God's family. Paul is explaining the difference between the old life that saw us opposed to God and the new life in Jesus that sees us united with God. In our original condition we had every reason to be afraid of God and His utter Holiness.

So, the first truth for today is this, now we are in Christ we don't ever have to be afraid of God because we are not in our original condition! Read with me the same passage from Romans again, but this time from the Message Bible,

> *This resurrection life you received from God is not a timid, grave-tending life. It's adventurously expectant, greeting God with a childlike "What's next, Papa?"*

What Paul is saying is "We don't have to be afraid of who God is because He has put something inside us that means we need never be afraid of Him". We literally have a spirit of total confidence placed in our hearts at the point of adoption by the Holy Spirit. However sometimes Christians are secretly afraid because they feel somehow God is displeased because they don't measure up. Remember, God knows we mess up but His love for us is unconditional. While God requires wholeheartedness, He does not require success in being perfect, He knows we are dust.

If you struggle with the truth of your adoption, read this passage from Isaiah 53.

Surely, He has borne our griefs and carried our sorrows; Yet we esteemed Him stricken, Smitten by God, and afflicted. 5 But He was wounded for our transgressions, He was bruised for our iniquities; The chastisement for our peace was upon Him, And by His stripes we are healed. 6 All we like sheep have gone astray; We have turned, every one, to his own way; And the LORD has laid on Him the iniquity of us all Isaiah 53:4 (KJV)

Prayer,

Father help me today by your Holy Spirit to understand more fully what it means to be adopted as your child. Help me to walk in the full realization of this glorious truth day by day.

Benefits of Adoption

> Romans 8: 15 *For you did not receive the spirit of bondage again to fear, but you received the Spirit of adoption by whom we cry out, "Abba, Father."16 The Spirit Himself bears witness with our spirit that we are children of God, 17 and if children, then heirs; heirs of God and joint heirs with Christ, if indeed we suffer with Him, that we may also be glorified together.* (NKJ)

Looking at the subject of being adopted into God's family we have seen that adoption means that we don't need to fear God if we are in Christ. Today we will look at a profound but mysterious truth within adoption. I say mysterious because it's not possible to put your finger on it but nevertheless it is very real and dynamic bringing great peace to the human heart. In the believer there grows a personal conviction deep down inside that we are children of God. We don't learn it, we don't earn it, it's the mysterious deep-down assurance that the Holy Spirit gives us, we know that we know that Jesus is our saviour!

God has this silent way of speaking to His children. It's called assurance, it's unspoken yet powerful enough to withstand all of life's pressures if we choose to walk in its truth.

1 John 4:13 *By this we know that we abide in Him, and He in us, because He has given us of His Spirit.* (ERV)

Christ's death is more than just a historical event. It dealt forever with the sin that separated you from God. Our disobedience was dealt with on Calvary by Jesus and because of God's actions the believer can rest in the assurance He gives us.

> *But when the time arrived that was set by God the Father, God sent his Son, born among us of a woman, born under the conditions of the law so that he might redeem those of us who have been kidnapped by the law. 5 Thus we have been set free to experience our rightful heritage. 6 You can tell for sure that you are now fully adopted as his own children because God sent the Spirit of his Son into our lives crying out, "Papa! Father*! Gal 4:4 (Message)

Are you walking today in the reality of the peace and deep-down assurance of your adoption?

Prayer.

> Father thank you for your salvation and acceptance of me into your family. I praise you for the deep-down assurance that I am a child of God. Help me to walk today in this truth.

Adoption and a glorious privilege!

As we continue today with adoption there is something we don't often hear preached or expounded on, but Jesus promised us troubles. Oh dear! Strangely, one of the glorious benefits of our adoption into God's family is that we can expect to suffer at times.

> *I have told you these things, so that in me you may have peace. In this world you will have trouble. But take heart! I have overcome the world.* John 16:33 (NIV)

There is no avoiding this unpleasant truth. Some people are so taken up with "living in victory" that they bypass this pathway to blessing. There are two reasons adopted children of God experience unavoidable struggles at times. The first is that suffering is part of the human condition and Jesus experienced this more than anyone else, scripture says,

> For *we do not have a high priest who is unable to empathise with our weaknesses, but we have one who has been tempted in every way, just as we are--yet he did not sin* Heb 4:15 (NIV)

If our elder brother Jesus suffered, why should we be exempt?

The second reason is that in a strange way the Lord in His lovingkindness uses our difficulties to help us to mature, grow spiritually and glorify His name. Remember the words the Lord spoke to Ananias concerning Paul's future suffering,

I will show him how much he must suffer for my name. Acts 9:16 (NCV)

Sometimes the Lord uses our struggles like a megaphone to call us closer to Him in order that we might rediscover the peace and strength only He can give. He does not always change our circumstances but He does change our hearts. In this way suffering can be a pathway to blessing. Paul said,

> *...and if children, then heirs; heirs of God and joint heirs with Christ, if indeed we suffer with Him, that we may also be glorified together* Rom 8:17 (NKJ)

The truths of adoption are gloriously manifold, and what some people see as negatives God always sees as a positive. This is because there is no identity with Christ without partaking of His sufferings and there is no growth without pain. This means there is no perfection of our character without God chipping away at all that spoils us.

So today if you encounter struggles or suffering, stand firm in your faith and submit to the Lord's love and compassion for you. Remember Jesus said "*I will never leave you nor forsake you*" Today take heart, He has overcome the world!

Prayer,

Father I humbly come before you in this quiet moment. You know my circumstances and you know my heart. I surrender all of my struggles and stresses to you. Work in me for your glory, ease my burdens and please give me the grace and strength to hold your hand tightly today. Amen

Day 4

The Power of our Words

A word fitly spoken is like apples of gold in pictures of silver. Prov 25:11 *(KJV)*

I guess we all know the power of words and our text today talks about the ability of our words to bless rather than destroy. No one seems to know with any certainty what these words actually refer to but they do seem to have been a proverb in Old Testament, a bit like we would say "A rolling stone gathers no moss" Whatever origin and practice these words may be referring to, the central theme is this, words can be beautiful and bring emotional richness to a person.

Just thinking of golden apples hanging in a frame or on a platter of silver brings up in my mind thoughts of richness, sweetness and perfection and that is what today's verse is intended to do.

Solomon seems to be saying, a word spoken in love and sweetness at the right time to a person brings richness. Yet so often our words can do the very opposite. They can be harsh, cutting or just thoughtless on our part. For the Christian that is just not appropriate. Jesus always spoke truth in firmness but never without love and kindness. Someone said to me once "I always say what I think" and I thought to myself, it would be better to think about what you are saying! Words can bless but they can also wound deeply; it all depends on the heart of the person speaking the words.

Our mandate as disciples is to show the love of Jesus to all those we meet and, dare I say it, live with? I remember something the poet Maya Angelou said, "People will forget what you said, people will forget what you did, but people will never forget how you made them feel."

What will our words be today? like apples of pure gold resting on a silver platter in someone's life or will that person carry in their memory thoughts of how negative you made them feel? Our words never die because the eternal Lord listens, but He also forgives if we ask Him to.

Prayer

Father forgive me if I have used foolish words, cleanse my heart and let me speak with the love and tenderness that Jesus spoke with. Help me from now on Lord so that my words will be like Apples of Gold in pictures of silver in someone's busy and perhaps broken life. Amen

Day 5

We Reflect His Light

But you are a chosen generation, a royal priesthood, a holy nation, His own special people, that you may proclaim the praises of Him who called you out of darkness into His wonderful light. 1 Peter 2:9 (NIV)

For many people salvation tends to be seen in the light of sins forgiven, peace with God and an eternal home in heaven. While these things are obviously true, there is a deeper and much more profound mystery in salvation's story. You don't often hear teaching on this neglected truth but our passage teaches us that because we reflect Jesus, we are by our very presence in the world proclaiming the praises of the triune Godhead. This a deeper and more profound truth than just what the believer gains from their salvation. So today we are thinking about the amazing revelation contained in this simple passage of Scripture. As believers, all the truth spoken of here applies to each one of us whether we realize it or not. Peter chooses his words wisely, "chosen, royal priesthood, called and wonderful light" He does this to demonstrate that we are indeed God's precious possessions.

As Christians we all have part in God's eternal plan of redemption. It's not found in having a notable ministry or being successful, no! Our part in God's redemption is just being who we are! Let me explain.

When we are born again we are gathered into God's personal family and so have become a new creation through this spiritual birth,

Therefore, if anyone is in Christ, the new creation has come: The old has gone, the new is here 2 Cor 5:17 (NIV)

We have been literally transferred out of the kingdom of darkness into the kingdom of God's Son, this means we have been made heirs of God and joint heirs with Christ. The Christian life is multifaceted with many ministries, roles and focuses, but behind all that we see, feel and engage in God is doing something hidden from our eyes that is mysterious and mind blowing in its enormity even in me the weakest saint.

He is using us to declare to the world, the devil, demonic forces and indeed the whole of creation, His marvellous grace, in that the Lord, the three times Holy God should love and redeem through the cross, we who were hell deserving sinners.

His intent was that now, through the church, the manifold wisdom of God should be made known to the rulers and authorities in the heavenly realms Eph 3:10 (NIV)

Our salvation is beyond what we see, feel and understand; it springs from God's eternal councils, achieving His eternal purposes which is to declare openly and eternally His glory and righteousness through His redeemed people, and that's you and me!

Prayer

Father, I am amazed that you should be using me in this way. I stumble and falter yet you love me with a love that is so great that it declares just how glorious and powerful your grace is in me! Amen

The power of listening

Now the king of Aram was at war with Israel. After conferring with his officers, he said, "I will set up my camp in such and such a place." 9 The man of God sent word to the king of Israel: "Beware of passing that place, because the Arameans are going down there."............ 10 So the king of Israel checked on the place indicated by the man of God. Time and again Elisha warned the king, so that he was on his guard in such places. 11 This enraged the king of Aram. He summoned his officers and demanded of them, "Will you not tell me which of us is on the side of the king of Israel?" 12 "None of us, my lord the king," said one of his officers, "but Elisha, the prophet who is in Israel, tells the king of Israel the very words you speak in your bedroom" 2 Kings 6:8-18 (NIV)

Today we will think about listening to the Spirit's voice. In this genuine piece of biblical history, Elisha demonstrates a spiritual truth that will benefit all of us if we take it on board. It makes you smile though that the poor king of Aram could not even talk in his bedroom without Elisha knowing what was said! Not that Elisha was at the keyhole of course, but the Holy Spirit was telling him of the conversations and Elisha was listening. This was only possible because Elisha had cultivated the art of listening to the Spirit's voice.

Every believer has the potential to listen to the Spirit's voice, it's our birth right as Christians but we need to cultivate an ear to listen. The Spirit never says anything contrary to the word of God but He does plant seeds of vision and hope and He does give guidance. I would suggest that Elisha listened with wisdom mingled with faith and that is exactly what we must learn to do. We must be on our guard against mistaking our emotions and inner wishes for the voice of the Spirit. This will stop us from going off at a tangent and being so heavenly minded that we become of no earthly use! Over the years I have seen so many excesses and biblically wrong concepts and practices, simply because people say "the Lord told me" so we need to be shrewd just as Jesus said,

> *I am sending you out like sheep among wolves. Therefore, be as shrewd as snakes and as innocent as doves* Matt 10:16 (NIV)

What voice do you hear today? Is it the voice of doubt or fear? Or is it the still small voice of the Spirit? So often the world with its pressures and noise drown out the voice of the Spirit and when we allow that to happen it is to our detriment.

Why not take time today to be still and ignore the clamours around you and begin again to cultivate a listening ear? The ability of Elisha to listen brought enormous problems to the enemies of Israel! That is where we will pick up tomorrow.

Prayer,

Father, I do love and worship you, but sometimes I don't have the patience or ability to stop and listen to your voice. Forgive me for being too hurried and busy and give me the grace to walk with you listening to your still small voice. Amen

The Power of Listening

*Now the king of Aram was at war with Israel.
After conferring with his officers, he said, "I
will set up my camp in such and such a
place." 9 The man of God sent word to the
king of Israel: "Beware of passing that place,
because the Arameans are going down there."
.... 10 So the king of Israel checked on
the place indicated by the man of God. Time
and again Elisha warned the king, so that he
was on his guard in such places. 11 This
enraged the king of Aram. He summoned his
officers and demanded of them, "Will you not
tell me which of us is on the side of the king of
Israel?" 12 "None of us, my lord the king,"
said one of his officers, "but Elisha, the
prophet who is in Israel, tells the king of
Israel the very words you speak in your
bedroom."* 2 Kings 6:8-18 (NIV)

Yesterday we looked at Elisha and the way he was
used by the Lord to confound the enemy. To have an
ear that has the ability to hear from the Lord can
sometimes have ramifications that go far beyond our
personal lives or sphere of influence. Many years ago,
I heard the voice of the Spirit prompting me to begin
a work in India. We started with nothing and today
there is a thriving Bible Seminary that trains young
men and women to take the Gospel all over India, a
children's home and various churches. We never
know what God may do with us if we listen to Him.

Today we can be encouraged by how Elisha's tuned ear had the ability to bring real trouble to Israel's enemies. Remember we, as Christians, are salt and light in the world and no matter how we may feel or how we may be attacked, each one of us is a grain of salt and a ray of light. The devil was mortally wounded by Jesus at the cross and each grain of salt irritates him and reminds him of his end! How much more so when we listen to and obey the Spirits voice in our daily lives.

Later in the story we see how through his listening and faithfulness Elisha was able to ask the Lord to open his servants' eyes to what was really going on in the heavenlies,

> *And Elisha prayed, "O LORD, open his eyes so that he may see." Then the LORD opened the servant's eyes, and he looked and saw the hills full of horses and chariots of fire all round Elisha* 2 Kings 6:17 (NIV)

If we could see the heavenly armies that surround us because we are grains of salt and rays of light our perspective on our circumstances would change for the better!

Prayer,

> Father thank you for giving me the same opportunities to listen as Elisha had. Teach me to be still and step back from all the hustle and bustle in my life and help me to train my ear to your dear voice. Amen

The Power of listening

> *Now the king of Aram was at war with Israel. After conferring with his officers, he said, "I will set up my camp in such and such a place." 9 The man of God sent word to the king of Israel: "Beware of passing that place, because the Arameans are going down there."............... 10 So the king of Israel checked on the place indicated by the man of God. Time and again Elisha warned the king, so that he was on his guard in such places. 11 This enraged the king of Aram. He summoned his officers and demanded of them, "Will you not tell me which of us is on the side of the king of Israel?" 12 "None of us, my lord the king," said one of his officers, "but Elisha, the prophet who is in Israel, tells the king of Israel the very words you speak in your bedroom."*
> 2 Kings 6:8-18 (NIV)

Today we draw to a close our thoughts on Elisha and his ability to listen to the voice of the Spirit. God uses men and women with a "different spirit' who are willing to listen to and obey His promptings. Interestingly such people gain an idea of God's perception of things rather than just their own! What a difference that makes!

Elisha was living with the Lord's perspective, Angels were around him because the Lord had sent them. This he knew in his heart because of his grasp on God's perception but that was not the case with his servant. So, there is a clear distinction between Elisha and his servant, one knew but the other thought he knew! Even though the servant lived close to Elisha that did not confer the Lord's perception to him, he needed to learn to hear for himself. Of course, we know that Elisha prayed for him and his eyes were opened, can you imagine his shock and awe when he saw things from God's perspective! Perhaps Elisha smiled to himself!

> Don't be afraid," the prophet answered. "Those who are with us are more than those who are with them."17 And Elisha prayed, "Open his eyes, Lord, so that he may see." Then the Lord opened the servant's eyes, and he looked and saw the hills full of horses and chariots of fire all around Elisha.
> 2 Kings 6:18 (NIV)

Today keep trying to listen to the "still small voice" in your heart, always test against the scriptures anything to may feel the Lord is saying and don't jump to conclusions. Take time to put things on the back burner and ask the Lord to confirm it to you. Remember God is never in a rush, His time never runs out because He owns time!

Prayer,

Father teach me to be like Elisha and open my eyes till I see the things you are familiar with, help me to see your hand and hear your voice. I surrender myself to your gracious instruction. Amen

Grace in Persevering

> *You need to persevere so that when you have done the will of God, you will receive what he has promised. 37 For, "In just a little while, he who is coming will come and will not delay." 38"But my righteous one will live by faith. And I take no pleasure in the one who shrinks back." 39 But we do not belong to those who shrink back and are destroyed, but to those who have faith and are saved* Heb 10:36 (NIV)

We all go through times when we feel "low" or not quite up to the mark and I want to share with you today something the Lord showed me when I was having just such a day. After a very busy life of pastoring and teaching, in my retirement I was feeling unproductive, and to be honest, a bit of an appendage! It was then the Lord directed my eyes to the passage of scripture above.

Of course, this passage should not be taken out of its context and we don't have space here to expound on that, but it would be helpful to read the whole chapter and grasp the context.

There were two things the Lord impressed on me that day.

The first is, wherever I am now I need to persevere because that is where the Lord has put me! Often my objections to where I am are because I fail to see any self-perceived success. Yet as long as I am not living in sin or disobedience then God's favour is on me, but how can that be if I feel unproductive or low or even depressed? Let's think about that. What is it that makes us favoured by the Lord?

Well, Paul said "persevere" not because the effort of persevering would bring favour but because perseverance is the fruit of His Grace in our lives.

God's Grace on us manifested through Calvary, is God's approval of us and makes us eternally favoured in His eyes.

> *For he chose us in him before the creation of the world to be holy and blameless in his sight. In love* Eph 1:4 (NKJV)

The second thing the Lord showed me was this. It's not that my perseverance brings favour, it's because His Grace is "His favour" and that gives me the ability to persevere, and there is a massive difference.

Our text today tells us that time is very short. *In just a little while, he who is coming will come and will not delay.* This is a reality many Christians don't seem to live in.

Yet Jesus will return one day soon! And so, the remaining time we have left to us needs to be spent living in our faith and enjoying God's favour and Grace in our lives. Today, take a few moments to thank God for His abundant Grace in your life and enjoy being His disciple!

Prayer,

Father, thank you for your Grace poured freely into my life, thank you that You favour me and that the work of my saviour on the Cross gives me the assurance that the things you have promised will be mine in eternity. Jesus please return very soon! Amen

Day 10

Conforming

Do not conform to the pattern of this world, but be transformed by the renewing of your mind. Then you will be able to test and approve what God's will is, his good, pleasing and perfect will Romans 12:2(NIV)

I wonder if you have ever looked longingly at today's celebrities and thought "I wish I could be like them" Or "I wish I had their money!" Our culture is peppered with the rich and famous, but for them, behind closed doors life may not be all it seems! People can rise to stardom and notoriety overnight, but it can fail just as quickly.

So why is today's reading centred around celebrities and not being conformed to this world? Well for one simple reason. Sometimes, as Christians, the world's culture presses in on us to the point that, without realizing it, we are silently being persuaded to conform to its ways. Sadly, this leads to a dethroning of Jesus in our hearts. This is in direct conflict with what scripture teaches us. The message bible puts our text today ever so clearly!

Don't become so well-adjusted to your culture that you fit into it without even thinking. Instead, fix your attention on God. You'll be changed from the inside out

In the same way that water dripping on a stone will wear a hole in it over time, if we are not on our guard, the world's low standards eat into our Christian life and witness. Whether it's music, entertainment, interests, food or whatever, without realizing it we can subconsciously begin to follow our interests. When this happens, those things become like celebrities in our lives. Remember the scripture says we can be too well adjusted to the world!

For believers there should be only one celebrity in our lives, Jesus. He immeasurably outshines all of this world's prominent figures and culture, there are no photos of Him, He made no films or recordings, He wrote no books and He has never been on TV. Yet His fame and influence transcend this world and touch worlds we don't know about. Strangely one of the most amazing things about Jesus is that although He exercises so much influence, by and large, people don't want to recognize or believe He exists, what a paradox?

So, a couple of simple questions to close today, "Who sits on the throne of your heart? Who do you want to emulate? If your answer is Jesus then another question has to be, are you willing to submit everything in your life to the authority and control of Jesus who is after all heaven's eternal celebrity?

Prayer

> Jesus, forgive me if I have allowed something else to take your rightful place in my life. Help me to walk worthy of my calling and to be a good witness to you and your great Name! Amen

Redeemed Beyond Measure

Can you imagine giving birth to a son and then calling him "Mephibosheth"? especially when you know that the name has negative connotations. This name is made up of two Hebrew words, *paah*, which means, "to break into pieces, or shatter," and *bosheth*, which means "greatly ashamed, and "confusion. Why not take a few moments and read the story of the latter part of his life for yourself?

> *David asked, "Is there anyone still left of the house of Saul to whom I can show kindness for Jonathan's sake?2 Now there was a servant of Saul's household named Ziba. They summoned him to appear before David, and the king said to him, "Are you Ziba?""At your service," he replied.3 The king asked, "Is there no one still alive from the house of Saul to whom I can show God's kindness?"Ziba answered the king, "There is still a son of Jonathan; he is lame in both feet."4 "Where is he?" the king asked. Ziba answered, "He is at the house of Makir son of Ammiel in Lo Debar."5 So King David had him brought from Lo Debar, from the house of Makir son of Ammiel.*

When Mephibosheth son of Jonathan, the son of Saul, came to David, he bowed down to pay him honour. David said, "Mephibosheth!" At your service," he replied.7 "Don't be afraid," David said to him, "for I will surely show you kindness for the sake of your father Jonathan. I will restore to you all the land that belonged to your grandfather Saul, and you will always eat at my table."8 Mephibosheth bowed down and said, "What is your servant, that you should notice a dead dog like me?"9 Then the king summoned Ziba, Saul's steward, and said to him, "I have given your master's grandson everything that belonged to Saul and his family. 10 You and your sons and your servants are to farm the land for him and bring in the crops, so that your master's grandson may be provided for. And Mephibosheth, grandson of your master, will always eat at my table. 2 Sam 9:1 *(NIV)*

Briefly the context is that king Saul was dead and David had ascended the throne.

St Augustine said, "The New Testament lies hidden in the Old Testament and the Old Testament is unveiled in the New Testament" in this part of Old Testament history, we see St Augustine's words exemplified because there is a complete picture of the redemption we have through the Lord Jesus, albeit in the Old Testament culture and customs.

Remember though, later in the scriptures, King David is shown to fall into sin and commit murder when he took another man's wife. This just shows us that all flesh is prone to sin yet God still uses people when their hearts are right and at this time David's heart was right.

Mephibosheth was a broken man both by birth and physical accident. He even lived in a worthless place, Lo Debar. Two words make up the name of the barren place he lived," lo" which means "nothing" and "dober", which means "no pasture" and the whole name comes from a root word, which means "no promise." The poor chap was seemingly broken on all fronts! What future could he look forward to? Poverty and probably death at the hands of King David's soldiers.

Perhaps you feel a bit like a Mephibosheth at times; dry, no future, disadvantaged or even broken; but we are going to see that the very act of coming to the King in submission opens the way for blessings beyond measure.

Tomorrow we will look into Mephibosheth's experience at the hands of king David who was the forerunner of Jesus.

Prayer

> Father, help me to see the truth that you are a loving, gracious king who, when you look at our brokenness, sees the person that you love and that my Jesus died for.

The King!

Yesterday we looked at Mephibosheth and his disadvantaged lot in life. We saw that to state that he had a dismal future was rather an understatement.

Today we are looking at the other player in this drama, the King who could not have been in a greater contrast to poor old Mephibosheth. David, King of Israel, all conquering, having seen Saul and his wicked way defeated is now presiding over the people God had given him.

So often we can lose sight of the fact that outside of our personal world there is a different experience waiting for us. The bible records twice that David was called a man after "God's own heart" The first time was by Samuel who, speaking of the rule of Saul, said,

> *"the Lord has sought out a man after his own heart and appointed him ruler of his people,"*
> 1 Sam 13:14 (NIV)

This was referred to by the Apostle Paul when he said

> *God testified concerning him: 'I have found David son of Jesse, a man after my own heart; he will do everything I want him to do.*
> Acts 13:22 (NIV)

So, it's not surprising that David acted differently to any other king in that culture in order to show mercy. Instead of doing the usual thing which would have been to kill Mephibosheth and his family, David wants to bless him! That's God's heart coming through.

King David, the forerunner of the Lord Jesus, calls this poverty-stricken cripple to the royal palace. Can you imagine how Mephibosheth felt when he was finally ushered into the presence of the King?

Today, whatever your life may bring you, however real and exciting your walk with the Lord may be, or conversely however low you may feel, remember there is always a new experience around the corner when you come into the presence of the King.

Today remember that the one who has the power to restore is, because of His grace, your friend and He will always respond to you when you come into His presence.

Prayer

> Father, I choose to come into your presence today, expecting to meet with you and experience your restoring power and love in my life throughout this day.

Majestic Grace

Yesterday we looked at Mephibosheth's experience of coming into King David's presence, poor, frightened and broken. Today we see the difference true grace makes.

> *Don't be afraid," David said to him, "I will surely show you kindness for the sake of your father Jonathan. I will restore to you all the land that belonged to your grandfather Saul, and you will always eat at my table."*
> 2 Sam 9:7 (NIV)

God's grace knows no bounds and is foreshadowed in this amazing record from history. Mephibosheth deserved nothing according to his background and the culture of his day, yet the King bestowed on him things he had never dreamed of. Suddenly King David's grace reached into this broken man and restored to him the inheritance that Saul had forfeited.

I guess that within a few moments Mephibosheth became one of the richest men in the nation! He did nothing to deserve it, nothing to merit it, grace just did it!

But King David was not finished, *"and you will always eat at my table"* No more scratching a living in barren Lodebar.

Now every meal would be a feast, he would share from the same table the food that the King ate

David's grace to Mephibosheth was amazingly lavish, wildly extravagant and all encompassing. It was given and not earned or merited. This is just the way the Lord deals with His people. Background, experience, lack of experience, ability or lack of ability have nothing to do with how God deals with us.

The grace we receive was earned and paid for by Jesus on the Cross of Calvary. However, we should note that Mephibosheth knew he was broken and admitted his condition to the King.

> *Mephibosheth bowed down and said, "What is your servant, that you should notice a dead dog like me?"* 2 Sam 9:8 (NIV)

This broken man humbled himself, admitted his condition and in bowing down submitted himself to the King.

This is the pathway to blessing and receiving the Grace that the Lord Jesus offers. So often we major on ourselves, our wants and needs and we can be full of self-justification, but when before the king on our own, perhaps even on our knees, when we admit our condition and let our guard down, His grace and acceptance can be ours in abundance.

Why not spend a few moments and again surrender yourself to the Father of Grace, seek His forgiveness and blessing again then go out into the day with your hand in His.

Prayer

Father, just as Mephibosheth bowed down before King David, I too bow before you. I surrender again to you by an act of my will, take me, fill me, use me and make me a blessing to others today.

Redemption!

Today as you take a few moments with the Lord and reflect on our thoughts over the last few days, just let your God given imagination work on the scenario we have been looking at. In your mind try to imagine the scene. King David, perhaps on the royal throne, attended to by servants with his personal military guard, with the backdrop of all the finery of the King's residence.

Imagine by contrast Mephibosheth being ushered in, dressed poorly, no doubt using crutches, hobbling on his deformed feet with only disgrace in his lineage because of his grandfather Saul. He did not know the King's intentions that because of of David's regard for Jonathan who was Mephibosheth's father that David would bless him.

Can you imagine what the servants and guards were thinking? Perhaps something like get that beggar out of here, better still put him to the sword and be done with him. Poor Mephibosheth! So out of place, ill at ease and obviously very frightened by the royal decree.

Then David speaks,

> 2 Samuel 9:6 *When Mephibosheth son of Jonathan, the son of Saul, came to David, he bowed down to pay him honour.*

David said, "Mephibosheth!" "At your service," he replied. 7 "Don't be afraid," David said to him, "for I will surely show you kindness for the sake of your father Jonathan.
NIV

This must have come like a bolt out of the blue to Mephibosheth. He must have struggled to take in what the King was saying. The "man after God's own heart" was about to dispense grace in such abundance.

Now let your imagination think about our Saviour King Jesus and His royal intentions to you. He does not look at us and deal with us in accordance with what we deserve, nor does He evaluate us according to our ability to perform or always "get it right" He deals with us like King David in His bountiful Grace. In short, today the King wants to bless His children, nothing else.

Take some time today to revisit in your memory all that Jesus has done for you and given you since you first trusted Him. Be thankful and lift your heart in gratitude to the shepherd of your soul. He loves to bless but He loves to see our gratitude!

Prayer

> Father thank you for your Grace towards me, for all of your rich blessings that are mine through Jesus my saviour.

Day 15

Fear

I sought the LORD, and he answered me; he delivered me from all my fears. Psalm 34:4(NIV)

I well remember when I first began my ministry and had to preach as the pastor in a church to a real live audience, that before each message I would be racked with a sense of impending failure! "Why would anyone want to listen to you" said the fearful dark voice in the back of my mind. Well that was a long time ago and thank God I overcame that dark fear and managed to last 50 years preaching. That said it still tries to get my attention on occasions, but I don't entertain it. So, there is victory and hope over fear if we look for it in the right place.

While some people don't spend too much time thinking about it, for others it can dominate their whole approach to the Christian life, just the way it did me. Remember fear stifles us and draws us away from the things of God. Fear often breeds a sense of a greater fear that God is somehow displeased with us. Someone said "Fear is the birthplace of stress and anxiety, it generates emotional pain" I wonder which category you fall into? Have you gained victory over fear or does it grip you at times? The world is full of good books for Christians on self-help and methods of overcoming problems but sometimes I think we make things much too complicated!

The psalmist being human struggled with fear at times and yet he gave this simple yet perfect solution,

> *I sought the LORD, and he answered me; he delivered me from all my fears.* Psalm 34:4 (NIV)

I have found over the years of my ministry that a fear pondered on is magnified out of all proportion, but a fear given over to the Lord with sincerity and rejected by an act of my free will is fear that has lost its teeth!

So today if fear discourages you or dominates you at times, simply give that fear to the Lord. That sounds way too simple, surely there must be more to it than that? No! Jesus wants to be the master of all our fears, be they real or imagined, but we must come and surrender everything again to Him. Before you pray today's, prayer take a little time to think about what you are going to do and still your heart before the Lord of Peace.

Prayer,

> Jesus, I bring to you my fears of (name your fears out loud) I exercise my will to surrender them to you right now. Take my fear and give me peace instead of the torment this dark voice taunts me with in Jesus Name! Amen.

Complete in Christ.

For though I am absent from you in body, I am present with you in spirit and delight to see how orderly you are and how firm your faith in Christ is. 6 So then, just as you received Christ Jesus as Lord, continue to live in him, 7 rooted and built up in him, strengthened in the faith as you were taught, and overflowing with thankfulness. 8 See to it that no-one takes you captive through hollow and deceptive philosophy, which depends on human tradition and the basic principles of this world rather than on Christ. 9 For in Christ all the fulness of the Deity lives in bodily form, 10 and you have been given fullness in Christ, who is the Head over every power and authority. Col 2:5-10 (NIV)

What wonderful words to ponder on over the next couple of days,

For in Christ all the fulness of the Deity lives in bodily form, and you have been given fullness in Christ, who is the Head over every power and authority.

Many believing people can sometimes feel incomplete in one way or another, either lost dreams, feeling distanced from Jesus or just unsure of where they stand in God's eternal purposes.

Paul is telling us that as believers we are not left to our own devices, in fact we have all the fullness of Christ to live in and draw on. Today in Christ is everything we need, strength for each battle, grace for each new difficulty, forgiveness for each failure, in fact everything, spiritually, emotionally and physically is found in the fullness of Jesus Christ that has been given to us. Literally all we need for the time we spend here on earth is found in Jesus our saviour.

Making the step from feeling incomplete in some way to knowing the security and abundance in Jesus involves repeated steps of faith and a working knowledge of God's word that feeds our spiritual lives. Feeding on the word and taking steps of faith means we get to know Jesus so much better and the more we know Jesus the more we understand the Father. This is because Jesus is the only person who has shown us and told us what the Father is like. Only through Jesus can the Father be approached. Remember it does not matter if we have been believers for a hundred years, there is so much more to learn and grasp through Jesus, He is literally inexhaustible!

Do you feel incomplete in some area of your life? Jesus alone is the answer. The father wants to take you beyond your potential in relationship with Himself not just up to it through your relationship with Jesus. What step of faith are you willing to take today? Perhaps the most important step any of us can take is to venture afresh into God's word and allow it to instruct us.

Prayer

Father I want to step out into a greater relationship with Jesus and enjoy all the fullness you have placed in my Saviour. Forgive me when I feel incomplete because faith tells me I am complete in Jesus, so please help to have the strength today to live in that reality. Amen

Complete in Christ.

For though I am absent from you in body, I am present with you in spirit and delight to see how orderly you are and how firm your faith in Christ is. 6 So then, just as you received Christ Jesus as Lord, continue to live in him, 7 rooted and built up in him, strengthened in the faith as you were taught, and overflowing with thankfulness. 8 See to it that no-one takes you captive through hollow and deceptive philosophy, which depends on human tradition and the basic principles of this world rather than on Christ. 9 For in Christ all the fulness of the Deity lives in bodily form, 10 and you have been given fullness in Christ, who is the Head over every power and authority. Col 2:5-10 (NIV)

Yesterday we looked at Paul's words about being complete in Christ Jesus. We saw that the antidote to feeling incomplete was to draw closer to Jesus through the Word, this coupled with our conscious steps of faith brings us to a greater understanding of our heavenly Father. Paul is always encouraging us to look up and walk daily in Christ.

So then, just as you received Christ Jesus as Lord, continue to live in him, rooted and built up in him, strengthened in the faith as you were taught, and overflowing with thankfulness. Col 2:6 (NIV)

Being complete in Jesus means living in the deep assurance of the Fathers love to the point that other negative influences are being drowned out. Through our relationship with Jesus, the Holy Spirit reveals the deep things of God in ever amazing ways.
Learning that we are complete in Jesus leads to joy which in turn leads to a thankful heart that overflows with praise. Sadly, however, it's possible to overflow with problems when we allow them to push Jesus out.

What is overflowing in your life today? Is it joy as you draw closer to the Father and learn more of your Saviour's love? Or do negative influences threaten your peace? Don't allow problems to overflow but let the joy of the Lord be your strength. We are already complete in Christ because that was secured for us at Calvary! Sometimes however we must take conscious steps of faith and dig into the word in order to be nourished and overflow with Jesus.

Prayer

Jesus please help me to learn afresh the glorious truth that I am complete in you. Thank you for Calvary and thank you for accepting me, even though I don't deserve your acceptance. By your grace I will dig into your word and take steps of obedience and faith today. Amen

Day 18

Losing and Gaining

What good is it for someone to gain the whole world, yet forfeit their soul? Mark 8:36 (NIV)

This question posed by Jesus to His disciples and the listening people is one that most of us will be familiar with. We tend to think of this question in the sense that, if we gain the riches of the world yet ignore God, then our future in eternity is bleak, meaning our eternal soul loses its future in heaven with Christ. This is perfectly right but there is more to Jesus' words than that.

Many people spend so much of their time getting, earning and so on, and this means that all our efforts can go into feeding and caring for our physical lives. Thus, we don't have any time to nurture our inner person or our souls.

Being very practical about it we can sacrifice very positive things that really enrich our lives. Things like friendships, a good night's sleep, worship, rest and relaxation, personal prayer, family life and service for others. We can lose positive qualities in our souls in real time. The results are that we are overworked, stressed and far less than we could be. Not only are our day to day lives impoverished, we can lose eternity with Jesus.

A vital question for us today is where do I place the emphasis in my life? Of course, a busy single mother with children trying to work, juggling her time with school, work and the home, or a busy executive with heavy responsibilities will never feel that they have time for anything other than the demands of the day. That's just the way life is, so everyone reading this will know this tension and probably to a very great extent.

That said, each one of us has to start somewhere! Remember it's not in the length of time we give in a day to Bible reading or prayer, it's where our hearts truly take refuge. Out of that refuge, when we can take just a few seconds to breath our hearts to Jesus comes a tiny and an indefinable assurance of His presence, no matter how busy we are. This naturally begins to nurture our souls, yes in a very small way but as we grow in breathing our hearts to Jesus so the nurture in our souls also grows.

Adopting these principles in our lives no matter how busy we are naturally leads to more time with Jesus, opportunities to read His word and a desire to pray in a deeper way. There will be opportunities that we don't see now but will be opened up to us by the Holy Spirit. Admittedly you may not see the way ahead at the moment, but give the Holy Spirit a chance!

Prayer

> Lord I am so busy, many, many things clamour for my time and attention. You know that Lord,

but I want to feed my soul on you. Please help me to grow in you and give me moments in my day when I can be at peace and in communion with you Lord. Amen

Direction of Flow

*So now there is no condemnation for those
who belong to Christ Jesus. 2 And because
you belong to him, the power of the life-giving
Spirit has freed you from the power of sin that
leads to death* Romans 8:1 (NLT)

Let's spend a little time today thinking about our
direction of travel. When we had our caravan, we
would get the opportunity to walk along the river's
edge. At times the flow of water would be a raging
torrent, at other times a mere trickle. It all depended
on what the weather had been doing the day before.
Something that all rivers have in common is to flow
in one direction, pulled inexorably by gravity to the
lowest point which is ultimately the sea. From the
river's point of view the flow can only ever be
forward, ever moving into new experiences, bends in
the river, boulders to flow over or around or the
experiences of wide-open river banks where the flow
is restful.

That is how our lives with Jesus are meant to be. New
exciting and stimulating days, always moving into the
new things God has for us. Sadly, however that is not
always the case because we can get tempted to flow
backwards!

What do I mean by that? Well, we all have yesterdays and for some people their yesterday can become enormous in their mind, perhaps much more so than is warranted. It's in our memories and thought processes that the past can lurk. When this happens, we begin to flow backwards, struggling with old hurt, failures or guilt. We are starting to move towards the hurt or pain again. For a Christian though these things actually belong in the sea of God's forgetfulness.

> *For I will forgive their wrongdoing, and I will never again remember their sins.* Heb 8:12 (CSB)

So, if a river flowed backwards it would break natural laws and in the same way when we relive and worry over past failures we break God's principles of forgiveness. Let's be clear on what forgiveness really is. When we come to the cross in repentance asking for forgiveness through His blood, there is no way He doesn't forgive us! Scripture is pretty explicit on this point

> *If we confess our sins, he is faithful and just and will forgive us our sins and purify us from all unrighteousness* 1 John 1:9 (NIV)

Of course, we also have to forgive ourselves but that's for our next reading!

Which way will you flow today? Forwards into new things with God enjoying His peace through forgiveness or will you hang on to the things God has dealt with?

The choice is yours but it's a shame to ignore what God has forgiven and just live in the shadows from yesterday that lurk around.

Prayer,

> Father, thank you for your unparalleled forgiveness to me, help me to move ever forward with you flowing in your direction of travel. Not being distracted by my yesterdays but enjoying today with you. Amen

Direction of Flow

So now there is no condemnation for those who belong to Christ Jesus. 2 And because you belong to him, the power of the life-giving Spirit has freed you from the power of sin that leads to death Rom 8:1 (NLT)

Yesterday we looked at the direction of our flow in the river of life. Do we flow forward with God or backwards to old problems, hurts and guilt? We saw that forgiveness is complete in Jesus but sometimes we have to forgive ourselves and that is not so easy!

So today I want to share with you some of my basic thoughts on self-forgiveness and negative experiences. The first is this, I may be a victim but it's me who chooses to live in the shadow of that, conversely, it's me that can choose to break free into the joy of my heavenly Fathers peace. This might be hard to accept because we can feel trapped and indeed our identity can be wrapped up in these things. Remember though, God never asks us to do something that we can't do, neither does He allow us to be in a place we can't escape from,

No temptation has overtaken you except what is common to mankind. And God is faithful; he will not let you be tempted beyond what you can bear. But when you are tempted, he will also provide a way out so that you can endure it. 1 Cor 10:13 (NIV)

To forgive myself I must first recognize my personal ability and responsibility to choose, this is paramount. In the same way that Jesus taught us to forgive someone who has wronged us, I must choose to forgive myself and then ask God's forgiveness for allowing myself to flow backwards into my past. There is always grace for us to forgive ourselves and others if we want to. It may seem impossible but our Father is the God of the impossible. It's always a personal action, choosing to forgive in order to be free from the past.

We are responsible for the choices we make and we can all choose to walk out of the shadows of yesterday, equally we can choose to remain firmly rooted in the past if we so wish, it's a choice we make. I know it's easy to write this and perhaps you are thinking "you don't know my circumstances". That's very true, but I have my own yesterdays and I know from experience that our heavenly Father knows all these things and has provided grace and strength through the Holy Spirit for us to walk free.

So today why not lay out before the Lord all the yesterdays that might be troubling you and seek His help as you choose to walk free in His strength?

Father,

Thank you for my freedom purchased by my Saviour on the cross. Help me to walk wisely in faith moving with the forward flow of your Spirit and not looking backwards but towards all you have for me. Amen

The Fear of the Lord

> *The fear of the LORD is the beginning of wisdom, and knowledge of the Holy One is understanding* Pro 9:10 (NIV)

The concept of "fearing" the Lord confuses some folks but is an enlightenment to others, so today we will ponder these words from King Solomon.

For the unbeliever, at least those who acknowledge there is a supreme being, the fear of God could well be the fear of judgment and death. It's true to say that in days gone by most people at least gave mental assent and acknowledged God even from a distance.

However, it seems that in our postmodern culture, a vast number of people just blank the concept of God and never seem to bother to think about eternity or any consequences for how they live. For them fearing God in any sense never becomes an issue although sometimes these changes when they feel they are approaching the end of life. This is why believers should take every opportunity to share their eternal hope.

For the believer the fear of God is something totally different. This is because there is a world of difference between fear in the negative sense i.e. being afraid of someone or something and the believers "fear of God", which is a very positive and healthy thing.

The believer's fear is three-fold, reverence, respect and honour for God, His word and His ways.

> *Therefore, since we are receiving a kingdom that cannot be shaken, let us be thankful, and so worship God acceptably with reverence and awe, 29 for our God is a consuming fire.* Heb 12:28-29 (NIV)

This reverence, respect and honour is the biblical "fear of God" for Christians. As we grow and mature in spiritual things this becomes a huge motivating factor for us to surrender more deeply to the King of Kings. The believers' "fear of God" has the effect of making us want to draw closer to Him and walk in ways that are more pleasing to Him. This is truly the beginning of wisdom that transcends all human understanding and logic making the wisdom of this world seem foolish! The wisdom that comes from a believer's "fear of God" affects everything carrying them through this life into eternity!

> *The fear of the Lord is the beginning of wisdom; all who follow his precepts have good understanding. To him belongs eternal praise* Psa 111:10 (NIV)

Do you have this healthy "fear of God" reigning in your life today? If you don't, begin to lift your reverence, respect and honour for the King of Kings higher in your life because it will have eternal consequences for you.

Prayer.

Father, I desire to honour you and lift you higher in my life, by your grace help me to grow in maturity and walk in a pleasing manner to you. Amen.

Your Personal Call From Heaven

Today we are going to begin thinking about Paul's words "called heavenward" please notice the alternative rendering in the NKJ "The upward call"

> *Not that I have already obtained all this, or have already been made perfect, but I press on to take hold of that for which Christ Jesus took hold of me. 13 Brothers, I do not consider myself yet to have taken hold of it. But one thing I do: Forgetting what is behind and straining towards what is ahead, 14 I press on towards the goal to win the prize for which God has called me heavenward in Christ Jesus. (NKJ the upward call) 15 All of us who are mature should take such a view of things. And if on some point you think differently, that too God will make clear to you. 16 Only let us live up to what we have already attained.* Phil 3:12-16 (NIV)

Scripture teaches us that the Father has called by name every believer in order that they might respond and become part of His family.

> *For he chose us in him before the creation of the world to be holy and blameless in his sight. In love* Eph 1:4 NKJV

Over the next few days we will think of this theme and it will bring home to us just how special we are to our Heavenly Father. Often, we allow daily cares and thoughts to crowd in on us and hide some of the precious truths of our faith.

Thoughts and cares, like our own low self-worth or feelings of guilt over failings, sadness over lost opportunities or just the struggles of daily temptations such as we all face. It's so easy in these circumstances to lose sight of very basic things, like God made me and knows me through even to the point of knowing that I will fail and yet, still loving me and providing a path to fresh forgiveness in Jesus.

These things can and do often obscure the "heavenward call" that Paul spoke about, but the truth is that God has personally called each one of us and over the next few days we will see the nature of our heavenly call.

So, as you start your day today, just take a little time to think about God calling your name from heaven! How personal and individual that call is and how unchangeable!

Prayer,
> Father it amazes me that you know my name, it is even more amazing to me that you have called me personally to Jesus and given me your forgiveness through Jesus' work on the cross. (Continued over)

Help me to walk through today feeling special in your eyes because that is what I am, your child, because you called my name. Amen

Your Personal Call From Heaven

Yesterday we looked at the concept of our heavenward call in Paul's words,

> *Not that I have already obtained all this, or have already been made perfect, but I press on to take hold of that for which Christ Jesus took hold of me. 13 Brothers, I do not consider myself yet to have taken hold of it. But one thing I do: Forgetting what is behind and straining towards what is ahead, 14 I press on towards the goal to win the prize for which God has called me heavenward in Christ Jesus. (NKJ The upward call) 15 All of us who are mature should take such a view of things. And if on some point you think differently, that too God will make clear to you. 16 Only let us live up to what we have already attained.* Phil 3:12-16 (NIV)

Today we begin to look at some specifics of our call by the Father. In the book of James our Father is called "The Father of Lights".

> *Every good thing given and every perfect gift is from above, coming down from the Father of lights, with whom there is no variation or shifting shadow* James 1:17 *(NASB).*

To be called heavenwards is the ultimate "good and perfect gift" and theology teaches us that it is God the Father who calls people to His son Jesus.

Don't be surprised at this, but the call from above originally came through Jesus from the "Father of lights". This is a great mystery because the Trinity is one, yet the Father, Son and Holy Spirit are three distinct personalities, perhaps in the same way that you and I are body, soul and spirit yet one person! There is no hierarchy in the Trinity; we usually put them in the order above just for convenience, but they coequally work together and are one.

Sometimes, as Christians, we fail to grasp the scope of the Gospel. We often have a woolly understanding of simply coming to Christ and being saved. Yet the bible teaches that in eternity the divine heart of the Trinity made great decisions and then each part of the Trinity began to play their part. This culminated in you and I at our salvation becoming convicted of our sin and submitting to Christ. We see this very clearly in,

Long ago, even before he made the world, God loved us and chose us in Christ to be holy and without fault in his eyes.

> *His unchanging plan has always been to adopt us into his own family by bringing us to himself through Jesus Christ. And this gave him great pleasure.* Eph 1:4 (NLT)

So, our call heavenwards is not based on our merits, abilities nor even on our own perceived worth, but on the wishes of "The Father of Lights" this gave Him great pleasure. If we are Christians it is because we have been called.

Prayer

> Father, thank you for calling me and providing the way to you through my saviour Jesus. Help me to always remember that not only do you love me but you are intensely committed to my well-being as I daily walk with you. Amen

Your Personal Call From Heaven

Not that I have already obtained all this, or have already been made perfect, but I press on to take hold of that for which Christ Jesus took hold of me. 13 Brothers, I do not consider myself yet to have taken hold of it. But one thing I do: Forgetting what is behind and straining towards what is ahead, 14 I press on towards the goal to win the prize for which God has called me heavenward in Christ Jesus. (NKJ The upward call) 15 All of us who are mature should take such a view of things. And if on some point you think differently, that too God will make clear to you. 16 Only let us live up to what we have already attained. Phil 3:12-16 (NIV)

Today we continue looking at our upward call. We have seen that it is the father who calls us to Jesus based only on His wishes and desires. But naturally that call needs to be communicated to us in a meaningful way and that is the wonderful work of the Holy Spirit. Do you remember when you first heard the Gospel? For most people it is hard to grasp and understand, let alone believe. This is biblical and normal in our fallen world.

But people who aren't Christians can't understand these truths from God's Spirit. It all sounds foolish to them because only those who have the Spirit can understand what the Spirit means. [15] We who have the Spirit understand these things, but others can't understand us at all. [16] How could they?
1 Cor 2:14 (NLT)

It is due to the gracious work of the Holy Spirit that the Father's call to us is illuminated into a reality in our hearts. The Holy Spirit opens our spiritual eyes so that we gain a sense of conviction of sin and a consciousness of the majesty and Holiness of God. This is called conviction, it comes at different times and in different ways to different people but in the end, it is the work of the Holy Spirit and without it there can be no salvation. Proof of His working in us is that we get an understanding of God's love that draws us to Jesus and enables us to respond.

It's also very interesting that the Holy Spirit never draws attention to Himself, He never seeks any glory for Himself but His ministry and role as a part of the Trinity is to draw attention to Jesus and to glorify Him. In this way he facilitates the call of the Father and opens human hearts to come to Jesus.
Just spend a little time today pondering on the ministry of the Holy Spirit in your life.

Prayer,

Father, thank you for sending the Holy Spirit to me to open my eyes to your great love and the sacrifice of Jesus on the Cross for me. Help me never to trivialise the ministry of the Holy Spirit because without Him I would not be praying today. Amen

Your Personal Call From Heaven

Today we close our subject of our upward call with a deep assurance!

> *Not that I have already obtained all this, or have already been made perfect, but I press on to take hold of that for which Christ Jesus took hold of me. 13 Brothers, I do not consider myself yet to have taken hold of it. But one thing I do: Forgetting what is behind and straining towards what is ahead, 14 I press on towards the goal to win the prize for which God has called me heavenward in Christ Jesus. (NKJ The upward call) 15 All of us who are mature should take such a view of things. And if on some point you think differently, that too God will make clear to you. 16 Only let us live up to what we have already attained.* Phil 3:12-16 (NIV)

So today we are looking at the culmination of our good and perfect gift from the "Father of Lights" This call from the Father in heaven is to go Heavenwards. In other words, we are called to go to the origin of the call. There is an old song that says "This world is not my home, I am just passing through"! So often we live and think as if this life is all there is to being a Christian, we get so taken up with the pressures and treasures of this life that we can lose the eternal perspective on things.

You see we are ultimately called to a heavenly home whose builder and maker is God. As Christians we are literally walking in the footsteps of Abraham,

> *It was by faith that Abraham obeyed when God called him to leave home and go to another land that God would give him as his inheritance. He went without knowing where he was going. [9] And even when he reached the land God promised him, he lived there by faith—for he was like a foreigner, living in a tent. And so did Isaac and Jacob, to whom God gave the same promise. [10] Abraham did this because he was confidently looking forward to a city with eternal foundations, a city designed and built by God.* Heb 11:8 (NLT)

Our upward call means that we can trust and know that there is a better day coming. When this earthly existence ceases as it will for all of us, we know that we look for something better because of the call of the Father, the facilitating of the Holy Spirit and the sacrifice of our Lord Jesus.

> *And God will open wide the gates of heaven for you to enter into the eternal Kingdom of our Lord and Saviour Jesus Christ.*
> 2 Peter 1:11 (NLT)

The glorious but sometimes forgotten truth about our call is that it will not be changed!

Calls from heaven are never rethought, never made by mistake and they never fail because they are like the Father who made the call, eternal. This means our future is eternally secured! Remember the verse we read from James a few days ago?

> *Every good and perfect gift is from above, coming down from the Father of the heavenly lights, who does not change like shifting shadows* James 1:17 (NIV)

When we remember these things and dwell on them, all the problems and discouragements we face fade into the background, eclipsed by the magnitude of our Father's love and His eternal call. Today step back and listen to the Spirits assurance of your personal call to Jesus Christ.

Stand fast in Christ, all of heaven knows we have been called and the Father does not make mistakes!

Prayer,

> Father, thank you for your call to me personally, once again I surrender to you and ask that you will help me to gain a deeper understanding of all that you have done for me. I look forward to my heavenly home with you. Amen

Day 26

Blessed through Suffering.

We have no scripture for today and the title may seem contradictory, yet our title contains a very valuable spiritual truth. Perhaps a little story will help to explain what I mean.

On the 24th March 1820 little Fanny Crosby was born into a world of suffering. At six weeks old, she developed a cold and a local country doctor sadly prescribed a hot mustard poultice for her eyes! When the baby cried he said that the treatment was working and they should leave it. For poor baby Fanny the result was total blindness!

Yet in her disadvantaged life Fanny saw beyond physical things into eternal truths. She grew up to become one of the most prolific hymn writers in history, writing more than 8,000 hymns and gospel songs, and more than 100 million copies went into print. Believers all over the world today know and love hymns like "Blessed Assurance" "He hideth my Soul " and "Draw me nearer " to name just three that were born out of Fanny's suffering.

Concerning her blindness towards the end of her life Fanny Crosby reportedly wrote, "In more than eighty-five years, I have not for a moment felt a spark of resentment against him (the doctor), for I have always believed from my youth up that the good Lord, in His infinite mercy, by this means consecrated me to the work that I am still permitted to do."

Sometimes we can feel as though there is no way forward because of suffering or circumstances in our lives over which we have no control, yet Fanny Crosby demonstrated this profound truth, it's not really our circumstances that hold us back but the way we respond to them, our approach either holds or releases us!

What difficulties are you staring at today? No matter what they are, behind them and perhaps just out of your gaze is the smiling face of Jesus obscured by your preoccupation with the difficulties. Lift up your eyes and change your gaze, look heavenwards to eternal things and remember the old saying "Two men looked out through prison bars, one saw mud but one saw stars"

Beginning to look beyond the immediate does not solve all the problems instantly but it adds a new dimension and source of strength. Without any doubt, Jesus is always the answer.

Prayer,

> Father, thank you for your servant Fanny Crosby and the example she has left me. Please help me to see you through the mist when times are hard. Jesus, may your face ever come into greater focus in my life. Amen

God's Great Plan!

> *.........God, the blessed and only Ruler, the King of kings and Lord of lords, 16 who alone is immortal and who lives in unapproachable light, whom no one has seen or can see. To him will be honour and might forever. Amen*
> 1 Tim 6:15-16 (NIV)

Today we are starting a short look into this amazing text. Some of the points raised in this mini-series have been made elsewhere in this book but they are near to my heart and worth looking at from a different angle.

These words not only serve to underpin our faith but they can open up the way for us to glimpse eternal mysteries. So, we are going to take a bird's eye look at the method the Lord has used to redeem us to Himself.

First of all, remember everyone born since Adam has been subject to sin and its eternal consequences.

> Rom 3:23 *for all have sinned and fall short of the glory of God,* (NKJV)

However, the bible teaches us that in the councils of eternity before time and creation, the Lord devised within the Trinity a plan of salvation for our sinful condition. Which if you think about it raises some really interesting questions for debate but not for today!

> *For he chose us in him before the creation of the world to be holy and blameless in his sight. In love 5 he predestined us for adoption to sonship through Jesus Christ, in accordance with his pleasure and will*
> Eph 1:4 *(NIV)*

Our text tells us that God the Father lives in *"unapproachable light"* obviously with the Son and Holy Spirit, because they are the Trinity. This is born out in the OT,

> *"you cannot see my face, for no one may see me and live.* Exodus 33:20 (NIV)

And confirmed by Jesus,

> *Not that anyone has seen the Father, except the One who is from God; He has seen the Father* John 6:46 (NIV)

So, there is no denying that the Father dwells in impenetrable light and is utterly hidden from human eyes, this means that to us He is invisible! Perhaps this is something you have not thought of. Another interesting thought is that even if He did not live in impenetrable light, we still could not see the Holy Father because of our sin!

Sadly, people often reduce the Father to a human level in their thinking so that they can understand Him, but this degenerates Him and while I understand the sentiment and motive it is not wise. We can lose the sense of His majesty and eternity and this in turn impacts our faith and hinders our growth. Always remember the Triune God is totally beyond our understanding.

> *"For my thoughts are not your thoughts, neither are your ways my ways,"* declares the Lord. Isa 55:8 (NIV)

Beyond doubt the Godhead is a mystery to human minds but this is clear, God's great plan is woven intricately by the Trinity and includes the Father, Jesus the Son and the Holy Spirit in equal measure but that's for tomorrow. For today, think about this truth, the Father dwells in *"unapproachable light"* and that's where Jesus and the Holy Spirit come into God's great plan for us.

Prayer

> Lord I confess there are great mysteries in your word, but for today I want to dwell on your utter glory, I cannot envision what unapproachable light may really mean but in humble faith I submit to the mystery of who you are and I rejoice in my salvation Amen.

God's Great Plan!

> *.........God, the blessed and only Ruler, the King of kings and Lord of lords, 16 who alone is immortal and who lives in unapproachable light, whom no one has seen or can see. To him will be honour and might forever. Amen.*
> 1 Tim 6:15-16 (NIV)

Yesterday we looked at the words *"unapproachable light"* as pertaining to God the Father. Today we will think of the part that the Son plays in our salvation.

We saw that the father is veiled in *"unapproachable light"* and hidden from us because of sin. In the OT, Job greatly lamented the fact that God was beyond his reach and that someone was needed to bridge the gap between God and man,

> *If only there were someone to mediate between us, someone to bring us together,*
> Job 9:33 (NIV)

This is exactly what Jesus has done, He has shown and declared the Father to us and in so doing through Calvary bridged the gulf of the Fathers *"unapproachable light"*

"I am the way, the truth, and the life. No one comes to the Father except through Me. "If you had known Me, you would have known My Father also; and from now on you know Him and have seen Him......Have I been with you so long, and yet you have not known Me......... He who has seen Me has seen the Father... John 14:6-11 *(KJV)*

Jesus, totally God yet totally human, Jesus our saviour, part of the Trinity walked this earth and laid down His life to appease the Holiness and justice of His Father. The debt has been paid and the devil's power has been smashed! This is a great mystery and is the heart of the everlasting Gospel.

When Adam sinned, he offended the holiness and justice of God. Today when people deny God's existence they too offend His Holiness, when they say "it's my life I can live how I want" they are offending the Lordship of God the creator. I guess I am guilty of this in some measure but thank God when I fail and repent I have a mediator who represents me to the Father.

> *For there is one God and one mediator between God and mankind, the man Christ Jesus,* 1 Tim 2:5 *(NIV)*

The Trinity's great plan of salvation had intricately woven into it the willingness and ministry of the Son,

> *Then I said, 'Here I am--it is written about me in the scroll-- I have come to do your will, my God.'" Heb 10:7* (NIV)

Jesus through Calvary has opened the way for all men to be forgiven if they repent!

Prayer

> Jesus my redeemer, you have paid the price, you have bridged the gap and you have forgiven my sins, Thank you ! Amen

God's Great Plan!

………God, the blessed and only Ruler, the King of kings and Lord of lords, 16 who alone is immortal and who lives in unapproachable light, whom no one has seen or can see. To him be honour and might forever. Amen.
1 Tim 6:15-16 (NIV)

We have seen that sin is universal and blinds eyes and hearts to God, in fact it has made human hearts dead towards God.

As for you, you were dead in your transgressions and sins Eph 2:1 (NIV)

Yesterday we looked at the outworking of God's great plan of salvation as seen in the member of the Trinity Jesus, who was willing to come and pay the price for sin. This raises an interesting question, if hearts are dead towards God how can our salvation happen? Dead people can't choose what to do! However, this is where the Holy Spirit's ministry comes in.

Being part of the Trinity, the works of the Holy Spirit are many and varied but His main role is to draw attention to Jesus and His redemptive work on the cross. He convicts of sin and opens dead hearts, this in turn leads to salvation because He convicts us to turn to Jesus for forgiveness.

> *Godly sorrow brings repentance that leads to salvation and leaves no regret, but worldly sorrow brings death. 2 Cor 7:10* (NIV)

Without His ministry, seeing the cross in clarity, believing in Jesus and being regenerated by the Holy Spirit salvation is not possible.

So, scripture shows us that the Holy Spirit has many roles to play in the church. As we have said He regenerates by putting spiritual life where there is no life because of our sin. He also empowers believers for service and witness and then enlightens us as we look into God's word. Sometimes He does these things over a period of time, other times almost simultaneously. Everything the Holy Spirit does begins with His main role, drawing our attention to Jesus and His teachings,

> *But when He, the Spirit of Truth, comes, He will guide you into all the truth [full and complete truth]. For He will not speak on His own initiative, but He will speak whatever He hears [from the Father—the message regarding the Son Jn 16:13* (Amp)

Often people will say "Father, Son and Holy Spirit" as if that was their order of importance. We must not think like that, we have said elsewhere that the Father, Son and Holy Spirit are co-equal, three entities yet one God. That confounds our minds I know and many, perhaps someone reading this page, won't accept the doctrine of the Trinity but for me this is settled and revealed in scripture.

Without the glorious ministry of the Holy Spirit there could be no Christians and no salvation because we would all be in our natural state,

> *The person without the Spirit does not accept the things that come from the Spirit of God but considers them foolishness, and cannot understand them because they are discerned only through the Spirit.*1 Cor 2:14 (NIV)

The great plan of redemption involves all of the members of the Godhead. What a wonderful salvation we have, chosen, redeemed and sealed by the Holy Spirit.

> *And when you heard the word of truth (the gospel of your salvation)—when you believed in Christ you were marked with the seal of the promised Holy Spirit* Eph 1:13 (NET)

Yes, the blessed Holy Spirit shows us Jesus, opens our eyes to His work on the cross, imparts new life calls us to repentance and then seals our salvation. That's why as Christians we have that deep-down assurance of salvation.

Prayer.

> Jesus my salvation runs so much deeper than I sometimes feel. It humbles me to know that each member of the Glorious Trinity is one hundred percent involved in my salvation. Thank you, Lord Jesus.

Day 30

The King's Imminent Return

Always be ready. Otherwise he might come back suddenly and find you sleeping. 37 I tell you this, and I say this to everyone: 'Be ready!
Mark 13: 36 (NIV)

Our text exemplifies how every Christian should live their life, in the constant anticipation of the personal return of Jesus Christ! The great Dr. G. Campbell Morgan said, "I never begin my work in the morning without thinking that perhaps he may interrupt my work. I am not looking for death, I am looking for Him." What a thought!

Sadly, it is a fact that many believers don't want to think like that, they don't want to acknowledge that their lives may be interrupted in an irreversible way by the trumpet blast that heralds His return. Unspoken thoughts like "the end of the world hasn't come yet, so why think about it" or "probably not in my lifetime" can tend to dominate the subconscious. All that said it is an inescapable truth that Jesus will return,

> *After he said this, he was taken up before their very eyes, and a cloud hid him from their sight.10 They were looking intently up into the sky as he was going, when suddenly two men dressed in white stood beside them.*

> *"Men of Galilee," they said, "why do you stand here looking into the sky? This same Jesus, who has been taken from you into heaven, will come back in the same way you have seen him go into heaven."*
> Acts 1: 9 (NIV)

Our text today records the very words of the Master on the subject. You would not be reading this book if you did not believe in Jesus, so why not take Him at His word?

> *"I tell you this, and I say this to everyone: 'Be ready!'"*

Yes, the saviour of our souls is returning, no one can tell you precisely when this will happen but common sense tells us that this world cannot go on much longer as it is. The big question is "are you ready"? can you echo the sentiments of Campbell Morgan and say within yourself "I wonder if He will interrupt my day?

Make no mistake He is returning; the Father has a day set aside for that glorious event. Live in the reality of this truth, allow the excitement of possibly seeing Jesus face to face today or tomorrow fill you with joy. There is a lovely old hymn that has this refrain, "He's coming soon, He's coming soon, with joy we welcome His returning It may be morn, maybe night or noon--We know He's coming soon".

Are you ready?

Prayer

Lord Jesus, I long for your return, forgive me for being too busy to think about this glorious event. The thought of seeing you face to face fills me with great joy. Amen

What's in a Name?

Our world is full of celebrities, some are good role models and some have fallen. Sadly, even within the church, we have our willing or unwilling celebrities. Sometimes a bright figure will fall to the dismay of those who have put them on a pedestal and wrongly assumed they were faultless, sadly to the pleasure of those who want to criticise. It's good for us to remember no matter what our opinions of others are that all flesh is prone to fail and it is sobering to remember that Jesus said,

> *"Let any one of you who is without sin be the first to throw a stone at her.* John 8:7 (NIV)

However, there is a celebrity that outshines all the world's celebrities and will never fall nor will He ever fail us. There are no photos of Him, He is not found in films and no book was ever written by Him. Yet His fame and influence transcend this world we live in and surprisingly touches and reigns in worlds we don't even know about yet in the cosmos! The truth about Him is even more breath-taking when we begin to look at Him in detail. One of the most amazing things is that although He is such a celebrity exercising so much creation wide influence, yet He has personal time for every human being on planet earth! His name is Jesus Christ, eternal, omnipresent, all powerful and deeply desiring to welcome anyone who doesn't know Him into a profound life changing relationship with Himself.

Starting today and for the next day or so let's ponder His name.

> *Therefore, God exalted him to the highest place and gave him the name that is above every name,* Phil 2:9

> *"All authority in heaven and on earth has been given to me"* Matt 28:18

All names in the Bible have meanings and they often reveal something of the person's lifestyle or character. Examples taken from the OT could be, Noah = Rest, Elijah = My God is Jehovah, and Enoch = Dedicated. Therefore, it is reasonable to assume that Jesus Christ has a name that tells us something about Him. In fact, the bible is full of different names given to Jesus, simply because one name cannot express everything about Him in terms we can understand. Examples are,

> *"I tell you the truth, I am the gate for the sheep* John 10:7 (*NIV*) So one name of Jesus is the door.

> *"I am the good shepherd. The good shepherd lays down his life for the sheep.* John 10:11 (NIV) So another name of Jesus is the Good Shepherd.

> *"I am the Alpha and the Omega,"* says the Lord God, *"who is, and who was, and who is to come, the Almighty."* Revelation 1:8 (NIV) Again, another name of Jesus is the "first and last of everything" (please read the context)

All these names give us a tiny glimpse into just a part of the activities of our amazing divine saviour.

In closing today let's think about just one thing the Bible says about this amazing celebrity.

> *You believe that there is one God. Good! Even the demons believe that -- and shudder.* James 2:19 (NIV)

Just ponder today that Jesus, whose very name makes demons shudder is your Friend, Good Shepherd and Saviour. No wonder the bible tells us in whatever circumstance we are in we should be,

> *fixing our eyes on Jesus, the pioneer and perfecter of faith. For the joy set before him he endured the cross, scorning its shame, and sat down at the right hand of the throne of God. Heb 12:2* (NIV)

Prayer,

> Jesus my Lord and saviour, I feel overwhelmed when I think of who you are and the power and influence you have. I also feel so small and insignificant until I remember that you love me with an everlasting love. Thank you, Jesus!

What's in a Name?

Yesterday we touched on the world's celebrity culture and noted how Jesus manifests His influence not only in this world but in the cosmos as a whole. We noted that even demons' shudder and tremble at His name. We also noted that there are many names given to Jesus, each describing a facet of His role and ministry.

Yet there is an interesting verse in Revelation that tells us there is a separate name that exclusively encapsulates hidden qualities of Jesus that no one else knows!

> *"His eyes were as a flame of fire, and on his head were many crowns; and he had a name written, that no man knew, but he himself."*
> Rev 19:12 (KJV)

Among the many names He claims, Jesus has a name that only He knows and understands, whether this will ever be revealed to us I don't know! I personally think this refers to the fact that Jesus is utterly indescribable in His entirety and this secret name describes that indescribable quality.

To me, the unknown name must have been bestowed on Him by the Father and refers to His power and authority that is way beyond our human (and perhaps angelic?) ability to comprehend. I also feel that this means that when Jesus Christ returns to earth with His unknowable name along with His redeemed saints, His personality, power and actions that are reflected in this unknown Name will extend far beyond whatever humans can ever imagine! Matthew Henry the great Bible commentator says, "His perfections cannot be fully understood by any creature"

No wonder the Bible teaches that His Name is exalted!

> *Wherefore God also hath highly exalted him, and given him a name which is above every name*: Phil 2:9 NKJV

The next time we sing or read about Jesus being "high and lifted up" remember this is your saviour and your elder brother!

Prayer,

> Jesus I am in awe of you and I bow to you. You alone are my Lord and Saviour and I honour you to the very best of my ability. Amen

Day 33

Sharing His Yoke

Come to me, all you who are weary and burdened, and I will give you rest. Take my yoke upon you and learn from me, for I am gentle and humble of heart; and you will find rest. For my yoke is easy, and my burden is light." Matt 11:29 (NIV)

Perhaps today these words of Jesus do not readily resonate with us, simply because the Yoke is not something we see every day. It refers to a piece of shaped wood that couples two working animals together which of course means that their combined strength can be used. If we think of a harness used to keep Oxen moving forward together perhaps pulling a plough, as I have seen many times in India, then we will get the idea. The important thing for us in today's reading is this, the yoke means that the animals do not go their own way but the way the master directs them. Jesus used metaphors and illustrations that ordinary people of His culture could relate to.

Kristine Brown wrote on Crosswalk.com "The idea of a yoke around my neck isn't too appealing, but when we think about the yoke's purpose, we can see the beauty of the message behind it"

The real essence of our text's meaning is found in the writings of Matthew Henry the great Bible commentator who wrote,

"To call those who are weary and heavy laden, to take a yoke upon them, looks like adding affliction to the afflicted; but the pertinency of it lies in the word "my" "You are under a yoke which makes you weary: shake that off and try mine, which will make you easy."

We need to understand the context of the words of Jesus in our text today. In Matt 11:20-24 Jesus had been talking about sin and the suffering it causes, He then spoke in a kind of duel statement directed to His Father and the disciples simultaneously especially if you look at verses 25-30 in the NKJV during which He invited people to accept His yoke rather than the yoke of sin that men labour under.

So today for us as Christians our text is calling us to exchange the weight of problems we carry, perhaps caused by our own wrong decisions, disobedience or plain discouragement and weariness, surrendering to His total leadership and direction.

More importantly, if you have never given your life to Jesus, then He is inviting you right now to lay down the yoke of your old life and take His yoke on your shoulders. His yoke is not heavy but it is pleasant to carry, it brings peace to the soul and that is not possible without His yoke. Remember Jesus said, *my yoke is easy, and my burden is light!*

Will you accept the Master's invitation to take on His yoke if you are not a believer? If so, pray the prayer at the end of this page. If as a believer you desire to surrender more of your life to the Master, His invitation still stands, respond now!

Prayer

Jesus, I desire to accept your yoke into my life for the first time, I surrender my life to you asking you to forgive me and cleanse me in the work you did on Calvary. Amen.

(If you prayed this prayer please contact me on my Blog https://faithexperience.blog using the contact page)

For the believer,

Jesus, I gladly surrender more of my life to your yoke, give me grace to walk in your ways for your glory. Amen.

Our Father the Craftsman

Today we are going to think about the Divine Craftsman.

> *For we are God's workmanship, created in Christ Jesus to do good works, which God prepared in advance for us to do.*
> Eph 2:10 (NIV)

Do you ever think of yourself as God's workmanship? Sometimes we can lose sight of this truth and end up overshadowed with life and its struggles. Being God's workmanship means that God is working with His personally chosen material, that's you and me! And here is a thought to ponder on, we are the basic material He is using in our life because we are so special to Him! An earthly craftsman knows his materials, he has a plan and a design and he has the skill to bring into reality all his plans. All human creations have some form of function and the heavenly craftsman is no different.

Paul says that being God's workmanship naturally leads us to do good works. In addition to this Paul shows us a profound mystery that we can ponder today, our good works were ordained by God in advance of us! Not only does He plan for us and fashion us, He is working towards us being the finished article and He never fails!

To him who is able to keep you from stumbling and to present you before his glorious presence without fault and with great joy Jude 1:24 (NIV)

Perhaps you feel that God can never use you or that somehow you don't come up to the mark! but it's His faithfulness and power that achieves His will, not our endeavours. All we have to do is submit to His Lordship and be obedient.

So, do you feel like God is working in your life? If not, it's no matter because He always is. Sometimes our Father will use the strangest circumstances and situations to fashion us into the image of His son Jesus. That is what He has in store for you, the realization of the good works he has destined for you as a follower of Jesus.

And we, who with unveiled faces all reflect the Lord's glory, are being transformed into his likeness with ever-increasing glory, which comes from the Lord, who is the Spirit 2 Cor 3:18 (NIV)

Prayer,

Lord help me to grasp the truth that you have great works for me because of Jesus. I long to be presented faultless in your presence, so thank you Lord that even when I am not aware you really are working in me for your glory. Amen

Our Father the Craftsman

> *For we are God's workmanship, created in Christ Jesus to do good works, which God prepared in advance for us to do.*
> Eph 2:10 (NIV)

Yesterday we looked at the work that our Father is accomplishing in us and the resulting good works that can overflow our lives. Every craftsman will be familiar with the concept of a template. The dictionary defines a template as a "shaped piece of material used as a pattern in a manufacturing process, such as cutting out, or shaping." Our heavenly craftsman is at work in our lives and He is working to only one template and that is Jesus Christ.

Our Father never changes and while we may not understand the totality of one of His attributes i.e. Holiness, He is nevertheless the "three times Holy" God.

> *Each of the four living creatures had six wings and was covered with eyes all around, even under its wings. Day and night, they never stop saying:" 'Holy, holy, holy is the Lord God Almighty,' who was, and is, and is to come."* Rev 4:8 (NIV)

He is unchanging in His love and eternal in His methods of working in us to mirror the character and beauty of Jesus. The master craftsman dealt with Paul, Peter and John in the same way He deals with you and me. We are no less important to Him than the Bible characters that we read of, we are loved in the same way and His working is no less valid and efficacious in us than it was in them.

As the craftsman applies the template of Jesus in our lives through the operation of the Holy Spirit, little by little we change inwardly and this, in turn, leads to the good works that Paul refers to in our text today; good works, like the Fruits of the Spirit, acts of kindness to our fellow man, praying for our enemies and speaking of Jesus whenever we are given the opportunity. Very often these inner changes actually have an impact on the world around us and cause circumstances to change. These are the benefits of allowing the Master Craftsman to work in us but of course the real benefit is that Jesus is glorified in us.

Today, spend a little time talking to the Craftsman. Surrender again any areas that you can tend to withhold to His Lordship, and ask Him for forgiveness through the Blood of Jesus. Then invite Him again to work in you and bring to pass the good works He had prepared for you.

Prayer

> Father I surrender again to you, continue the good work of the Holy Spirit in my heart and life for your glory. Amen

Day 36

Read, Mark, Learn and Inwardly Digest

> *The unfolding of your words gives light; it gives understanding to the simple.*
> Psalm 119:130. (NIV)

The Message Bible has a refreshing way of quoting this verse,

> *Every word you give me is a miracle word how could I help but obey?* (Message)

The words of Archbishop Thomas Cranmer (1489-1556) when writing about the scriptures said "Read, mark, learn and inwardly digest" these words were used as a little mantra that I had to recite every day at one of the schools I went to as a child. Somehow it has stuck with me and ingrained in me the value of thinking about and noting everything I read in scripture to the best of my ability. So today I want to encourage you to think about your personal Bible reading and prayer

Reading the Bible is not always an easy thing to do and some people really struggle and then feel guilty or even give up if they feel they don't put in a certain amount of time. God does not want us to feel guilty, He just wants us to love Him because of what Jesus has done. Out of that love comes a desire to know more of Him, and as we have said elsewhere in this book that understanding is found in His word by the revelation of the Holy Spirit.

Segments of the church in days gone by have tended to make spiritual disciplines somewhat legalistic. I remember someone telling me as a very young believer that if I did not spend a certain amount of time each day reading the Bible and praying then I was failing as a Christian. This made me wonder if I might be losing my salvation! On other occasions I was put under pressure to go to all night prayer meetings because "that was the right thing to do as a believer" Thankfully those days have passed for the most part, but I do sometimes wonder about what has replaced them because I see so much superficiality in many who call themselves believers. All these spiritual disciplines have their right and proper place, but never in a legalistic sense. That was the problem with the religious leaders in Jesus' day.

Pray because you want to, cry out to God because you need to of course, but not at someone else's behest, let it come spontaneously from your heart at any time of the day or night. Walking with God is a perpetual relationship with Him; there is no set time table. If you struggle with your bible reading why not choose one of the Gospels, say Luke and read or listen to a chapter a day on your Bible app.

Physically reading or listening to one of the Gospels, especially if you use a red-letter Bible that highlights the words of Jesus, is your personal opportunity to literally delve into this most earth-shattering part of living history. Jesus originally bringing the Good news!

Reading or listening to what He said and did, understanding why and how he used miracles of healing to validate His words and learning its context allows your imagination to replay these events over and over in your mind. This can be a meaningful experience even for the mature believer and leads us naturally into adoration, praise and prayer.

If you struggle with reading and praying it's nothing to be ashamed or afraid of, it's a problem for many believers for different reasons. Remember, legalistic approaches lead to sterility. God has better things for you! Don't make up your mind to try harder, just relax and read or listen to the gospels, if a chapter seems daunting just one verse and meditate on that verse throughout your day. You will be surprised at how the Lord will speak to you.

Prayer.

> Lord, you know my weakness and the tendency I have to miss those things I should do. Lord Jesus I just want to expose myself to your word so that its entrance into my heart can bring new and exciting revelations by your Holy Spirit. Amen

Day 37

The Rough with the Smooth

> *Yet He knows the way I have taken; when He has tested me, I will emerge as pure gold.* Job 23:10 (NIV)

I guess every believer is familiar with the story of Job, righteous and rich only to become poverty struck and sick. Of course, what Job did not know was that he was just part of a twofold divine plan to demonstrate to the devil God's ability to restrict his plans. Job, in the dawn of history was, unwittingly, a prophetic picture of Jesus and how His righteousness would overcome and destroy the power of the devil once and for all at Calvary. In this sense, Job like Enoch and many other OT saints was prophetic.

Ignorant as he was of all the dynamics that surrounded him, Job clung on to his faith and utterly refused to let go! Even at his lowest point he remained firm,

> *His wife said to him, "Are you still maintaining your integrity? Curse God and die!* Job 2:9 (NIV)

I try to be practical in my writings and it's a fact of life that sometimes things are hard. I well remember a man who I had recently led to the Lord coming into the church heartbroken one day.

He had just been made redundant and was afraid to tell his wife. For a family with young children who were living on the edge this was disaster of the worst kind. I remember him saying between his tears, "what is God doing to me, what is He up to?" Of course, like Job he did not know the full dynamics surrounding his life at that point in time.

Many years have passed and yesterday I met this man as I went into church. He had never once turned his back on the Lord or doubted his new-found faith. Like Job, he hung on in there. Despite his problems the passing years have been kind to him and his wife simply because they hung on to the Lord. He had them in His grip just like Job. Their daughter, now married, sings in our worship group and their son-in-law helps run the large tech team.

You may be facing difficulties, fiery trials or just weariness and fatigue. Remember, hang in there like Job who knew that whatever happened to him "*I will emerge as pure gold*" as our text says. Just like Job, we don't know or understand all the unseen things that are going on in the spiritual realm around us but we do know that Jesus has our back!

Prayer,

> Jesus, thank you because you do have my back, I trust that all things in my life will work out for good and your glory because your word promises it. Give me grace and strength to be like Job and stand firm in you.

Lifted Up!

Who may ascend the hill of the LORD? Who may stand in his holy place?... 4 He who has clean hands and a pure heart, who does not lift up his soul to an idol or swear by what is false. 5 He will receive blessing from the LORD and vindication from God his Saviour Psalm 24:3 (NIV)

Today we are going to begin looking at David's comments in Psalm 24. He asks a question that he then answers for us. *Who may ascend the hill of the LORD? Who may stand in his holy place?... He who has clean hands and a pure heart,*

Sometimes I can read a verse like this and a dark voice whispers," well that lets you out then doesn't it?" How many times do we encounter something like this, only to begin to feel disappointment and a sense of failure, simply because we can fail so many times in a day. Well I certainly do! The other day when I was praying this dark voice said "you are so deluded, you think you know Jesus but really it's all in your mind" Often looking at scripture can surprisingly give the devil the opportunity to try and contradict God's word. He is never weary of looking over our shoulders and trying to discredit God's word!

When David answered his own question, he was speaking partly prophetically and he opened the way for us to see that clean hands and hearts are indeed possible but not in our own strength! See those words again from v5, *vindication is from God!*

Clean hearts and clean hands are only possible through Jesus and His work on the cross. Yes, we may feel sad at our failures and shortcomings, but our Father does not judge us for these things when we are believers. He knows we are dust and prone to fail because we were lost in sin and total depravity before God that Jesus came. He bore all our sin, failures and stumbles when He died for us.

Our part today is to surrender our life to Him and believe afresh in His atoning work. Yes, we will fail, we will get it wrong, perhaps even today, but our walk of faith tells us that all our failures are taken care of in Jesus, so our vindication comes to us through Jesus shedding His blood to atone for our sins and not our ability to never get it wrong.

Of course, this does not mean we can live as we like and not try to be obedient, of course not! we must try to live with clean hands and heart endeavouring to be a good example of our new life in Christ. But our security does not come not from our abilities but the cross and the forgiveness we have in Jesus! So today lift your eyes away from failure and gaze on the cross and all that Jesus has done for you.

Prayer,

Jesus, thank you for your atoning work on the cross for me, thank you so much for your forgiveness. Help me today to not see failure but the forgiveness I have in you. Also, Lord help me to be a good testimony to all around me so that others may see that cleanness that comes from you. Amen

Lifted Up!

> *Who may ascend the hill of the LORD? Who may stand in his holy place?... 4 He who has clean hands and a pure heart, who does not lift up his soul to an idol or swear by what is false. 5 He will receive blessing from the LORD and vindication from God his Saviour*
> Psalm 24:3 (NIV)

Yesterday we began to look at David's words in Psalm 24. We saw that cleanness comes not from our endeavours but the atonement of Jesus. We also noticed that there has to be an effort on our part to reflect all that Jesus has done for us in our day to day life so that we are a good example to others of Him.

Today we will look at what David had in mind when he said *"clean hands and a pure heart"* When he spoke like this he was thinking generally of the actions of our hands, not making a cup of tea of course! but the fact that the day to day condition of our life is so often revealed in the way we engage our hands. The actions of our hands are always motivated by the condition of our hearts which we will see in a moment. Hands in this context then refers to the actual things we say and do in our interaction with others. Clean hands enable us to have a good testimony of our saving faith in the Lord Jesus.

David also spoke about our hearts because he knew that our day to day words and actions reveal what is in our heart. So, a negative, critical or judgmental heart will be manifested in the words we speak and the actions we engage in. On the other hand, a loving, gracious, & forgiving heart is likewise manifested in words and actions. A clean heart is like clean hands and is the pathway to a good testimony for the Lord Jesus.

Our words, doing and thinking in life must be accountable to the Holy Spirit, and we need to learn to recognize His check in our spirit when things slip as they will! It's a sad thought though that we can become inoculated against His checking by our too busy or unclean lifestyle. That is why "clean hands and heart" are not just advisory but they are the test of our sincerity. Our hearts and hands matter!

Prayer,

> Father help me to care about the cleanliness of my hands and heart! Because I want to be a good witness for my Lord Jesus. Forgive me when I fail and enable me to learn from my mistakes and not stumble over them for your glory. Amen

Lifted Up!

Who may ascend the hill of the LORD? Who may stand in his holy place?... 4 He who has clean hands and a pure heart, who does not lift up his soul to an idol or swear by what is false. 5 He will receive blessing from the LORD and vindication from God his Saviour. Psalm 24:3 NIV

In continuing to think of David's words about clean hands and hearts, it helps to consider what our lives are planted in. Every plant in my wife's garden reflects the particular soil it is planted in. Some grow well and some do not, so their position in the garden is changed or the soil is adjusted until they thrive. Jesus said in a slightly different context,

> *If you grow a healthy tree, you'll pick healthy fruit. If you grow a diseased tree, you'll pick worm-eaten fruit. The fruit tells you about the tree* Matt 12:33 (Message)

What is the soil of our hands and hearts? This is important because we have seen that our outward life reflects what we are being nourished on inwardly. What is it that attracts and draws us in the secret part of our hearts I wonder? Because whatever it is will be influencing us.

One way or another our hands and heart reflect the fruit that we truly are. So, the kind and type of fruit in our lives as a very important issue for the believer.

The apostle Paul said,

> .... *for I have learned to be content whatever the circumstance* Phil 4:11 (NIV)

Learning to be content with our lot in life is wonderful soil to be growing in because we do not grow well on discontent but we thrive on inner peace and tranquillity. This in turn prompts us to rejoice in the Lord. That kind of inner peace and contentment colours how we act, think, feel and speak and it produces fruit. Other people then see in us something of Jesus as it shines out of us for His glory.

Why not spend a little time today thinking about the soil your heart is feeding on and then ask the Lord to help you adjust, so that you can thrive like a healthy plant in the Lord's Holy place. David asked, *Who may ascend the hill of the LORD? Who may stand in his holy place?* Standing in the Holy place is the reward of clean hands and heart" So it really does matter what we are growing in.

Prayer

> Lord thank you for all the potential you have placed in me, teach me to discern between the good soil and the not so good soil so that I may choose wisely and have "clean hands and a pure heart"

Day 41

Stumbling and starting again.

However, the hair of his head began to grow again after it was shaved off. Judges 16:22 (NIV)

The important thing in life is not failing, making mistakes or making wrong choices, because we are all prone to that! What is very important though is how we react after failing. We can beat ourselves up or choose to make amends and through God's grace get up and start again. There is no limit on how many times we might fail but neither is there any limit on how many times we can start again!

Our verses today are a prime example of God's forgiveness and a person's fresh start with the Lord.
Samson was the last of the judges of the Israelites prior to the monarchy and his history is in the book of Judges chapters 13-16. It's worth taking the time to read these verses.

The story of Samson is one of unparalleled physical strength and exploits, a man dedicated to God through God's choosing and the vow of the Nazarite, yet a man who succumbed to passion with Delilah and fell from his position. His strength was characterized by his long hair which Delilah cut off when he was asleep at which point he lost all his amazing strength. Samson was then captured and put into slavery by the Philistines.

He was blinded and was now totally humiliated, just because of what he did and said to Delilah. Thereafter he was forced to spend his time grinding grain for the Philistines. One day in the Philistine temple Samson was again made a laughing stock and humiliated even further, but God had not cast him off!

> *Then Samson prayed to the Lord, "Sovereign Lord, remember me. Please, God, strengthen me just once more, and let me with one blow get revenge on the Philistines for my two eyes." Then Samson reached toward the two central pillars on which the temple stood. Bracing himself against them, his right hand on the one and his left hand on the other, 30 Samson said, "Let me die with the Philistines!" Then he pushed with all his might, and down came the temple on the rulers and all the people in it. Thus, he killed many more when he died than while he lived.*
> Judges 16:28-30 (NIV)

So why are we reading this today? Simply to underscore two vital truths for present day believers. The first is this, our Father is a God of immense forgiveness. Samson's sin was a great failure but not outside God's willingness to forgive.

The second is this and you may not have ever thought about it, but the fact is it took time for his hair to grow again. Who knows how long it took, weeks, months perhaps years?

This tells us that when we fall, either in large or small matters it takes time for the restoration process to build and mature in our lives. Forgiveness is instant upon repentance of course, but sin leaves scars and they take time to heal.

So, Samson's hair growing again is meaningful, because it tells us that restoration is God's business. Again, we learn from this story that restoration is a process that takes time! So even after forgiveness has taken place, it takes time to rebuild spiritual disciplines in our lives.

Remember this glorious truth though, that after failing, God did use Samson again and He did it in a powerful way. Are you struggling with failure? Don't be downcast, look up and stand up, God still has a future for you, but the first step is always saying sorry and asking for forgiveness from the bottom of your heart.

Prayer.

Father, thank you that nothing can separate me from your love and power. I humbly ask forgiveness for any failure on my part and bring any sorrow I have to you asking for forgiveness and restoration.

Day 42

Importance of your work

> *Whatever you do, work heartily, as for the Lord and not for men, knowing that from the Lord you will receive the inheritance as your reward. You are serving the Lord Christ.* Col 3:23-24 (ESV)

I wonder how you view your occupation? Is it one of enjoyment or something that you must do, but there is something else you would much rather be doing?

Although it is not fashionable today to speak in such terms the bible places great emphasis on the importance of work ethics, both spiritual and temporal. *"Whatever you do..."* is a pretty all-embracing concept, it includes, family, work and leisure life. Jesus and His standards must invade every part of our life, that's the meaning of taking up your cross.

> *Then Jesus told his disciples, "If anyone would come after me, let him deny himself and take up his cross and follow me.* Matt 16:24 *(ESV)*

A good question for today is "does being a Christian impact the way I work?" In other words what is my work ethic?

You see, character and a work ethic are foundational for our Christian walk. Paul makes it very clear in today's text that we should be mindful not only of the quality of our work, but also our faithfulness to God in the way we pursue it. Of course, this embraces our witness while we are working. For many people today, work is just a means to an end, enough food on the table or extra money to give me the holiday I deserve. Such thinking will miss the biblical concept of work by a mile!

The concept of getting our hands dirty and working is a God given responsibility originally given to Adam in the garden of Eden.

> *The Lord God took the man and put him in the Garden of Eden to work it and take care of it.* Gen 2:15 (NIV)

In fact, the scripture goes much further when it says,

> *"For even when we were with you, we would give you this command: If anyone is not willing to work, let him not eat."* 2 Thess 3:10, ESV:

Remember though there is a world of difference between not being able to work and just avoiding it!

As Christians every task that comes our way should be viewed not as a drudge or a penalty but an opportunity to shine for the Lord.

Our text says *You are serving the Lord Christ.* Even if you feel like a square peg in a round hole in your occupation, take your eyes off the role and recognize that in its pursuit you are actually working for Christ and not for man. This approach to our work takes a conscious decision on our part and a leaning on God's grace to help us through occupational difficulties.

There is so much more I could write on this subject but sufficient to say when we put Jesus at the centre of our private and working life we are going to run into God's blessing you can't escape it!

Prayer,

> Lord I choose to honour you in my home and work life, endeavouring to do everything as if I were doing it just for you and no one else. Amen

Who are you walking with?

*And Enoch walked with God: and he was not;
for God took him.* Gen 5:24 (NKJV)

Enoch! Now there is a person from the early mist of
time to muse over! Yet his words and actions are
recorded in our Bibles today. There are so many
hidden jewels to be discovered in Enoch's life but for
today we will think of only one.

Walking with God is both mysterious and amazing!
Mysterious because we walk by faith trusting what
we can't see and holding a hand that we can't
physically touch. Yet amazing because the believer
"knows that they know" God's presence in their life
and as a result has the potential to have a deep and
supernatural peace about their relationship with their
creator.

Enoch's name means "dedicated" and Enoch walked
in faith for the 365 years of his life. It seems that no
matter what happened, he trusted and obeyed God
with the limited revelation that he had. Enoch's faith
filled heart literally caused him to walk with God.

Life is filled with so many distractions, family,
business, deadlines and so many other things that
demand our attention.

It's true that Enoch did not have computers, mobile phones or social media to contend with but I am sure that in his day and culture he had just as many distractions. Enoch was a godly man but he lived in a morally corrupt and wicked society. Even though men in the early days of history began to call on God according to Genesis 4:26, it seems that Enoch was the first man to uncover the true delight of daily walking with God. It seems he found something that even Adam didn't experience too much. He learned how to commune with God in every department of his life. When he had learned that skill the Lord made a graphic statement by taking him up to heaven.

Imagine 365 years having a growing relationship with God the creator. One can only wonder what depths of intimacy Enoch uncovered in these times. Remember God wants to walk with His friends. God used this relationship to make Enoch a prophet and in Jude v14 we read his momentous prophecy only to be fulfilled in the second coming of Christ.

> *Behold, the Lord comes with ten thousand of his holy ones, to execute judgment on all and to convict all the ungodly of all their deeds of ungodliness that they have committed in such an ungodly way, and of all the harsh things that ungodly sinners have spoken against him.*
> Jude v14.

As we close this daily reading notice I said that it was after Enoch's walk, prophecy and witness that God made an utterly profound statement. He literally took Enoch to heaven to wait until Elijah would join him!

Yes, God was working to a plan so he just took him! Enoch never did pass through the valley of the shadow of death but he went straight to Heaven.

I don't understand the way it happened, nor do I fully understand the state of Enoch or Elijah today, but "I know that I know" that God used His friend Enoch to demonstrate an unshakeable promise, "One day all who know me and walk with me will come to be with me where I am." Yes, even in the OT it was God's Grace that drew, accepted and communed with Enoch even though it was pre-Calvary.

In exactly the same way God's grace wants to draw us into a communing relationship even as you read this. Like Enoch Heaven can be our destiny because of Grace through Jesus Christ. Are you ready, have you tasted His grace?

So, it matters who we walk with today. Do we let the pressures of day by day life keep us from communing with God? Remember, it's not the amount of physical time that matters but the genuineness of our hearts in seeking to commune with our creator.

Prayer,

> Father, thank you for Enoch and the example he has left me. Help me to endeavour to walk as he walked, hearing your voice and sensing your presence. Amen.

Who are you walking with?

> *And Enoch walked with God: and he was not; for God took him.* Gen 5:24 (NKJV)

Yesterday we looked at Enoch's experience of walking with God and the unexpected way God used him. There is not much information in scripture about Enoch but what there is tells us a lot about his times and underlines the principle of walking with God. Enoch was the first man in the Bible who walked with God in this way.

> *after he begat Methuselah, Enoch walked with God three hundred years, and had sons and daughters. So, all the days of Enoch were three hundred and sixty-five years.* Gen 5:22–24 (NKJ)

Remember scripture shows us that God loves walking with His children. From the very beginning God had a relationship with Adam and Eve that found them together in Gen 3:8 "*walking in the garden in the cool of the day*". God created humans for the enjoyment of walking in relationship. God still longs to walk with His creation which is why His arms of grace pulls sinners into a relationship with Him through the Cross.

Perhaps we need to ask ourselves an important question again, who will I walk with today?

Some people are so busy and preoccupied that they feel justified in not prioritising a daily communion with God. It's true that God understands our situation but He also waits in the wings, sometimes trying to catch our eye with the troubles and workloads we have to contend with.

Let me encourage you to take just five minutes at some point today, still your heart and mind and reopen your life to the God who would love to walk through this day with you, no matter how life is for you at this moment.

Prayer.

Father thank you that through the death of your son Jesus on the Cross His arms are open wide to welcome me afresh into communion with you. Walk with me this day I pray, and let me experience a little of the peace and intimacy that Enoch had with you. Amen

Day 45

The way of Peace.

Let us therefore make every effort to do what leads to peace and to mutual edification
Rom 14:19 (NIV)

How often in life have we been the recipient of an unkind word or action? It happens all the time. Just the other day someone tried to scam us out of a sum of money, it made me angry and I must be honest in saying that lurking inside of me was that latent desire to "get even". I am sure we have all been there in one form or another, but then as in my case the Holy Spirit whispers "that's not the way of the believer is it? Have you ever noticed when the Lord checks you over something there is no way we can come up with anything to answer back?

We are called to a better way of living where we go out of our way to be at peace with others whatever the situation. Of course, there are times when standing for what we believe will cause tensions with others but everything we do and say should be presented in love. I personally have known many believers who had unbelieving partners who became so discouraged and frustrated because all their attempts to reach their spouse have met with a brick wall.

Often, but not always in cases like this their approach in the Gospel has been dictatorial, mildly aggressive and always harping on about what the other person needs to do to be saved.

I understand their loving motive but it's unwise to go about it in this way. No wonder the other party doesn't want to know!

In my first book Grace Before Grace (Amazon Books, online) I recount the story of a dear old saint whose husband had been aggressive to the gospel all their married life. Early into their marriage she wisely stopped "evangelising" her husband, just praying secretly and quietly for him. Many, many years later, towards the end of their married life together and just one month to the day before he died, Jesus stood at the foot of his single bed in the night and told Bert He loved him and died for him. Instantly Bert gave his failing life to Jesus and lived exactly one month. Why one month? Well you need to read the full story in Grace before Grace.

So, whether we are angry at someone or discouraged over an unsaved partner remember we are called ....to *make every effort to do what leads to peace and to mutual edification* as our text says.

Yes, we are called to show kindness, love and respect today in the face of whatever comes our way.

> *How beautiful on the mountains are the feet of those who bring good news, who proclaim peace, who bring good tidings, who proclaim salvation, who say to Zion, "Your God reigns!"* Isa 52:7 (NIV)

Prayer.

Father, please help me today to show grace, understanding and love in my interaction with people in all types of situations. Let me shine for Jesus and peace in this dark world. In Jesus Name, Amen.

Day 46

Spiritual Enlightenment

I pray that the eyes of your heart may be enlightened in order that you may know the hope to which he has called you, the riches of his glorious inheritance in his holy people, and his incomparably great power for us who believe. Eph 1:18-19 (NIV)

There is undoubtedly great benefit to us in being believers because of the grace of the Lord, and so we hopefully enjoy a daily foretaste of heaven in this life. Yet, even with this foretaste, life can have its rocky roads and bumps. This is why the life of the believer should be one of continual exploration as a result of new things being revealed to us by the Holy Spirit. It builds us up and strengthens us immensely. Very often these things happen when the Spirit momentarily opens the eyes of our understanding and pulls back a veil to allow us to peep within. Often these things are shown or uncovered in times of Bible reading or quiet reflection, or occasionally as in my case almost "out of the blue"

The whole point of Paul's comments in our text is to remind us of his prayer on our behalf. He prayed that we might experience this spiritual enlightenment day by day, so that our eternal hope will continue to grow.

Don't we all need a growing hope in this fragile world? So much distress, pain and conflict in almost every part of our globe. I often wonder how people with no hope in eternity manage to cope. I suppose it's by blotting out certain things that believers hold dear and refusing to accept the concept of eternity, and that's so very sad!

For believers, spending time with the Lord in His word has extremely positive results. Paul prayed that it would lead us to a deeper knowledge of our *"glorious inheritance"* i.e. the realities of Salvation, and a growing awareness of God's unfathomable power and greatness. These truths are part of the bedrock of certainty in our lives. There is an old hymn that says,

"We have an anchor that keeps the soul, Steadfast and sure while the billows roll, fastened to the Rock which cannot move, Grounded firm and deep in the Saviour's love" (Priscilla Owens 1812)

In reality Christ is our rock and anchor. He binds us to eternal things and Paul's prayer is that we will grow in our understanding of the personality of Jesus, the more we receive of the Spirit's revelation the stronger we become in our day to day walk.

Today, ask the Lord to open your eyes to further truths and mysteries, allowing His Spirit to guide you into deeper and richer things.

Prayer,

Father I humbly ask you to open my eyes that I might see rich hidden things in your words today. Strengthen me by your Spirit to walk in revelation every day with You. In Jesus Name, Amen.

Just Who is Jesus?

I, John, ...was on the island of Patmos because of the word of God and the testimony of Jesus. 10 On the Lord's Day I was in the Spirit, and I heard behind me a loud voice like a trumpet, ... 12 I turned around to see the voice that was speaking to me. And when I turned I saw seven golden lampstands, 13 and among the lampstands was someone "like a son of man", dressed in a robe reaching down to his feet and with a golden sash around his chest. 14 His head and hair were white like wool, as white as snow, and his eyes were like blazing fire. 15 His feet were like bronze glowing in a furnace, and his voice was like the sound of rushing waters. 16 In his right hand he held seven stars, and out of his mouth came a sharp double-edged sword. His face was like the sun shining in all its brilliance. 17 When I saw Him, I fell at his feet as though dead. Then he placed his right hand on me and said: "Do not be afraid. I am the First and the Last. 18 I am the Living One; I was dead, and behold I am alive for ever and ever! And I hold the keys of death and Hades.
Revelation 1:9-18 (NIV)

Today heralds slightly longer readings and sees the introduction to what we will look at in the coming days.

So, our next few days will be faith building and assuring, containing some elements of teaching.

Poor old John was exiled in poverty on the island of Patmos when he had his amazing vision. Notice it was on "the Lord's day" (perhaps we should go to church on a Sunday prepared to be surprised like John was!) Anyway, John saw Jesus standing in the middle of seven lampstands. These lamps are commonly considered to be representations of the church. This is because seven is God's perfect number and the church is perfectly complete with Christ in the centre. In the middle of the lamps was the risen Jesus. We know this from the way He was dressed and the things He said and did. I well remember my old Bible school principal labouring the point that Jesus was standing, showing He is proactive in His wider church. We all have some form of picture of Jesus in our minds. Something we were taught as a child, a likeness formed from the scripture or even a mental image from our favourite worship song or hymn.

However, in truth the reality, power and glory of Jesus is totally beyond our human minds to grasp, at least in this life. John was given just a brief glance and was utterly overwhelmed by what he saw.

John, to the best of his human ability and language, described in earthly terms the heavenly things he saw. Everything John described reveals something different about the nature, character and all surpassing glory of Jesus, and it left him utterly stunned!

Nothing contained in scripture is ever ad hoc or without meaning and it helps to remember that each of the different descriptions and revelations of Jesus found in both Old and New testaments give different glimpses into His indescribable personality, power and glory and we still don't grasp the enormity of our risen Lord.

So, over the next few days we are going to take a bird's eye view of just what John described.

Prayer.

> Father, help me to prepare my heart to look afresh over the next few days at my precious saviour. Thank you, Jesus, for being my saviour, please help me to get to know you more and more as we look at this passage

Just who is Jesus?

> *And when I turned I saw seven golden lampstands, 13 and among the lampstands was someone "like a son of man", dressed in a robe reaching down to his feet and with a golden sash around his chest.* Rev 1:12 (NIV)

Today we begin looking at John's vision of the "Son of Man" This is the title Jesus took to Himself and it refers to the fact that He was sinless humanity, Jesus was also identifying with suffering humanity such as we see prophesied in Isaiah 53. As God, He came down and lived among us, fulfilling the Law of Moses and doing what no other human being could ever do. In using this title Jesus was also linking Himself to Old Testament scriptures like, for example,

> *"In my vision at night I looked, and there before me was one like a son of man, coming with the clouds of heaven. He approached the Ancient of Days and was led into his presence* Daniel 7:13 (NIV)

There are many other examples in the Old Testament.

In his glimpse of the risen, glorified Jesus, John saw He was wearing a long robe with a golden sash around His chest.

No detail in scripture is ever meaningless so we can ask, why was Jesus dressed like this? Well, His long robe reveals Him as our High Priest.

> *Therefore, since we have a great high priest who has ascended into heaven, Jesus the Son of God, let us hold firmly to the faith we profess.* Heb 4:14 (NIV)

The Son of man, truly human and truly divine is our High priest. He alone has shed His blood for our redemption, He alone has become the atonement for our sins and presented it to the Father, and He alone intercedes for us daily. Our saviour is more than the sum of our mental pictures of Him, He is the Great High Priest of our souls.

Standing in the middle of the lampstands as Priest but also royalty shown by the golden sash, Jesus is revealed as King of Kings.

> *Then I looked, and I heard the voice of many angels around the throne, the living creatures, and the elders; and the number of them was ten thousand times ten thousand, and thousands of thousands, 12 saying with a loud voice: "Worthy is the Lamb who was slain To receive power and riches and wisdom, And strength and honour and glory and blessing!*

13 And every creature which is in heaven and on the earth and under the earth and such as are in the sea, and all that are in them, I heard saying: "Blessing and honour and glory and power Be to Him who sits on the throne, and to the Lamb, forever and ever
Rev 5:11 (NIV)

It's no wonder John was stunned! Totally overwhelmed by seeing the Jesus he knew from the days of His ministry on earth, the Jesus he watched go to Calvary and then rise from the dead, the Jesus he had talked to and touched. Suddenly seeing this same Jesus reflecting His worth and place in Heaven shook John to the core,

And when I saw him, I fell at his feet as dead
Rev 1:17 (KJV)

Prayer,

Father forgive me when I reduce Jesus to a level I can understand and fail to grasp some of the truths that John saw. Reveal to me through the Holy Spirit all the glory and truth that is "my Jesus" Help me to live according to His reality not my failings. Amen

Just who is Jesus?

His head and hair were white like wool, as white as snow, Rev 1:14 (NIV)

Yesterday we started to look at the details of John's vision of Jesus. Today we will move into another mystery that was revealed to John.

As John beheld Jesus he was struck with His hair. I like to think of the hair that John described as white being "brilliant white" like snow shining in the bright sun hard to look at! White was obviously not a sign of decay, but its brightness showed His eternity and utter purity, nothing but total righteousness and purity was shining from the hair of Jesus!

Sometimes we wonder why people do not seem drawn to Jesus, but in reality, His purity is foreign to sinful man. In His earthly ministry people hated Him without a cause to the point of killing Him on the cross. People are no different today, they reject Jesus because something in them recoils from His purity and divinity. This is the outworking of man's sinful nature. Outside of Christ, humanity is utterly corrupt and deserves only God's wrath because of sin. This is why we preach the Gospel, telling people that if they come to Jesus who died for them on the cross forgiveness will be given freely.

Such purity in Jesus and the Godhead is hard for us to comprehend. The New Testament says that one day all of creation will flee because of sin and corruption when confronted with God's purity.

> *Then I saw a great white throne and him who was seated on it. Earth and sky fled from his presence, and there was no place for them.* Rev 20:11 (NIV)

To believers though, His Lordship and Purity is a cause of great joy despite the condition of our world, this is because we know that right now Jesus is seated on the Throne with His Father. However, Jesus took things a step further when He said that one day He will be seated on His own Throne perhaps this will be on earth?

> *"When the Son of Man comes in his glory, and all the angels with him, he will sit on his glorious throne.* Matt 25:31 (NIV)

On a personal note I cannot write these things without being stirred in my spirit, I long for the day when I will meet Jesus as John did. My prayer for you as you read this is that you too will be stirred deeply and constantly turn your eyes heavenward.

Prayer,

> Jesus thank you for being my saviour, help me to grasp as much as I can your love, power and glory. Help me to be stunned like John at your brightness. Amen

Just Who is Jesus?

....and his eyes were like blazing fire
Rev 1:14 (NIV)

We are still looking at the vision of Jesus that John saw on the island of Patmos, we have seen His priestly robe and golden sash as well as His hair so white with purity and eternity that it was hard to look at. So today we will think about the eyes that John saw looking at him. Using his human words to describe heavenly things John records that "*his eyes were like blazing fire*

I would suggest that the eyes that once looked on suffering people when He healed them or raised them from the dead, the eyes that looked at Peter when he denied Him were somehow different now! John said His eyes were like an incredibly hot blazing fire! No detail in scripture should be overlooked so what can we take into our hearts today from John's description of the eyes of Jesus in this Patmos experience?

We sometimes say this or that person has piercing eyes, and we know what we mean by that but this was so different. The eyes that John saw pierced into his heart and soul. John instantly realised that nothing in him was hidden from these eyes. It's the same for us, the Lord Jesus looks not just deep into our heart and soul but right through us!

We are utterly transparent when He looks at us. When we understand this, it becomes impossible to justify any kind of sin and of course ridiculous to try to hide it. This is such a sobering thought, nothing I do, think, say, or desire is ever hidden from His eyes.

Another thought is striking here, the blazing eyes of Jesus are eternally looking with loving compassion on those who know Him and He looks out for them. We are never out of His protective gaze, He never blinks or looks away, we are the focus of His gaze. Why? because He eternally loves all those who have come to Him.

I would like to ask this simple question, "Have you come to Him? I ask this in the light of our third observation of these blazing eyes. The eyes of Jesus that impacted John are the eyes that will ultimately bring terror to wicked hearts and the souls of those who continually reject Him in this life.

Sometimes as Christians we can be guilty of sanitizing our concept of Jesus, turning Him into only a loving tender saviour which He is of course, but He has many other attributes. Jesus is co- equal with the Father and Holy Spirit. The Father says one day all His enemies will be made to bow to Jesus Christ.

> *The Lord said to my Lord, "sit at my right hand, Till I make Your enemies Your footstool.*
> Psalm 110:1 (NIV)

In the same way that there is no salvation except in the name of Jesus, so there is no other name anywhere either in heaven or hell that if exalted against Jesus will ever succeed. He is the ultimate King of Kings!

So, John's description of Jesus' eyes "blazing" is very apt and revealing in more ways than one. Today let's just spend a few moments considering how His blazing eyes should affect the way we live, speak and act.

Prayer,

> Jesus as I bow before you, I am willing to let your loving eyes, search my heart and soul. Reveal to me anything that does not please you and give me the grace to respond accordingly. Amen

Just Who is Jesus?

*His feet were like bronze glowing in a furnace………..*Rev 1:15 (NIV)

Today we continue our look at John's awe-inspiring vision of Jesus remembering that John could only describe in human language the heavenly things he saw. We saw the garment and sash, looked at his brilliant white hair and talked about His blazing eyes.

It seems as though when John saw the feet of Jesus he struggled to find fitting words. Its as though John said "His feet were amazing! Like molten bronze bubbling in the furnace, shining, so bright they were hard to look at." Again, we see the repetition of brightness and shining that was hard to look at. Molten bronze in a furnace is hard to fix your eyes on because of its brightness.

Remember Jesus was standing in the midst of the candlesticks, not beside but among them. The candlesticks as we have seen represent the church which is only the true church when Jesus alone is in the midst.

According to the second book of Samuel, when David defeated Hadadezer, bronze was considered a precious metal and a prize of war,

> *David took the gold shields that belonged to the officers of Hadadezer and brought them to Jerusalem. 8 From Tebah and Berothai, towns that belonged to Hadadezer, King David took a great quantity of bronze.*
> 2 Sam 8:8 (NIV)

Jesus appeared to John with bronze feet, standing in the middle of the lampstands. Bronze is a hard metal and in a biblical sense a precious metal.

Christ's victory on the cross over the devil is His authority for standing immovable and glorious in the middle of His church. The spoils of Calvary's conflict with the devil are now in the sole possession of Jesus!

According to my understanding, that's not the end of the story. If we look back to Isaiah 53 we learn that the spoils of Christ's Calvary conflict belong to Jesus and are shared with His sheep! I believe it was referring to the Father when we read,

> *11……..by his knowledge shall my righteous servant* (Jesus) *justify many; for he shall bear their iniquities. 12 Therefore will I* (The Father) *divide him a portion with the great, and he shall divide the spoil with the strong; because he hath poured out his soul unto death: and he was numbered with the transgressors; and he bare the sin of many, and made intercession for the transgressors.*
> Isa 53:11-12 (NJKV)

Christ's victory has become our victory, His "spoil" is shared with us, victory over death, forgiveness, eternal life and so much more. Sometimes we don't grasp how much Jesus has done and what has been given to us! Neither do we understand the glorious magnitude of our saviour. Today spend a little time musing on these things and from a grateful heart say "Thank you Lord".

Prayer,

Jesus I am overwhelmed by the glimpse of who you really are! Thank you for loving me, going to the cross for me and rising glorious from the dead. Hallelujah! Amen

Just Who is Jesus?

Over the past few days we have looked at John's vision of Jesus on Patmos. We have seen His robe and golden sash, His hair whiter than white, His eyes and feet of bronze and His voice like rushing water. We have not covered all that John saw, so perhaps you might like to muse on the things we did not say and make notes of your own thoughts.

Today we draw to a close by considering the response of John to such wonders and then the response of Jesus to John's awe. John records,

> *When I saw Him, I fell at his feet as though dead.* Rev 1:17 (NIV)

John's reaction raises many points that we can't think of here, some theological and some practical but if you would like to ponder further please contact me through my blog site for a more in-depth discussion.

In my book "Grace before Grace" A Pastors Life, (Amazon Books). I recount my own encounter with Jesus, it was of course quite dissimilar to John's but nonetheless just as earth shattering. We all come to know Jesus in different ways, some dramatic, some slowly on the journey through life but each true encounter will leave its mark.

> *Therefore, if anyone is in Christ, the new creation has come: The old has gone, the new is here!* 2 Cor 5:17 NIV

A true disciple of Jesus will display the fruit of the Spirit at least to some extent in their life but sadly, some claim to be disciples yet display no discernible fruit, please make sure you are not one of them!

John was so totally overwhelmed by what he saw he experienced a physical collapse, falling down to the floor of the cave or wherever he was. Totally overwhelmed by the magnificent transcendence of Jesus. Have you ever been overwhelmed when trying to look into the truth of your saviour? If not ask Him to reveal Himself to you afresh.

Remember, Jesus was still standing among the candlesticks yet we read,

> *Then he placed his right hand on me and said: "Do not be afraid. I am the First and the Last. 18 I am the Living One; I was dead, and behold I am alive for ever and ever! And I hold the keys of death and Hades.*
> Rev 1:17 NIV

How could this be? Unless Jesus bent down to touch him, perhaps on the shoulder, or on his head or hand in order to strengthen him. This is a wonderful point to make. Jesus still bends down to touch us the way He did John. Magnificence and humanity united, to impart from the Godhead to a fallen humanity acceptance and revelation of the Glory yet to come through His grace.

That's the gospel, the risen saviour who died on the cross and paid the price for our sins, now alive and reaching into the lives of all those who will come to Him. There is no greater message in the world!

Before we leave John today just consider the above verse but from the Amplified Bible,

> *"Do not be afraid I am the first and the last and the ever living one- I am living in the eternity of eternities. I died, but see I am alive for evermore, and I possess the keys of death and the realm of the dead!*

So back to the title of this series of daily readings, "Just who is Jesus?" Words fail me! What about you?

Prayer,

> Jesus, please draw me closer and reveal to me even greater wonders of just who you really are. I love and worship you and long for the day when you will come again or we will meet in glory. Amen

Day 53

How Little We Know!

However, as it is written: "What no eye has seen, what no ear has heard, and what no human mind has conceived" -- the things God has prepared for those who love him
1 Cor 2:9 (NIV)

The first word of our text is "however" this means that what follows should be seen in the context of what has already been said by Paul, so it would be beneficial to read the context in this chapter if you have time.

We all have a mental picture of the power and scope of the gospel as it pertains to us individually. This is usually a personal conclusion drawn from the sum total of our experiences in our walk, scriptures we have digested, messages we have listened to and books we have read. Our human minds are extremely limited when it comes to trying to understand God and His ways. If we understood all about Him, the reasons and the whys of the things He does, then He would not be God, would He?

It stands to reason therefore that our personal concept of our salvation is by nature extremely limited, not because of our lack of knowledge of the word, or personal intelligence but because of the limitations of human understanding, take for example,

For he chose us in him before the creation of the world to be holy and blameless in his sight........He predestined us for adoption to sonship through Jesus Christ, in accordance with his pleasure and will Eph 1: 4 (NKJV)

Do you really understand the full depth and meaning of this verse? I am not sure I do! These types of verses are commonly read by believers and passed over but what are the truths they contain? What does "Choose" "Predestined" or "Adoption" really mean? In what way do these words impact my concept of my salvation? What was Paul's motive in using such words? Sometimes we recognize a mystery and then just read on instead of stopping, pondering and asking the Lord to give us revelation about this or that truth.

Someone once said to me "Whenever I can't sleep I take the Lord's prayer and pray it through, I take it one or two words at a time, so "Our Father" becomes "Our" what does that word mean in this context? Is "Our" a universal "Our", or is it just confined to Jesus disciples? Does it include me? He said I ponder each word thinking it through, then I ask the Lord to share something with me about it. I always fall asleep before I have got very far but I learn a lot! Better than sleeping pills!"

Our salvation contains truths, mysteries and benefits that are well beyond our ability to grasp in this life, but if we dig we will be surprised at what we will find. The hymn writer wrote,

"Thy Word is like a storehouse, Lord, with full provision there, and everyone who seeks may come, its glorious wealth to share. Thy Word is like a deep, deep mine, and jewels rich and rare are hidden in its mighty depths for every searcher there". Edwin Hodder 1837-1904

Yes, so many, many indescribable truths, way beyond human understanding are ours through the work of Jesus on the Cross. Look forward to Glory, it will be an experience of eternal discovery!

Prayer

Father I am so glad my ways are not your ways, by faith I accept the exceeding great and precious promises that are mine through Jesus. Amen.

Day 54

Yes, Thorns are useful!

*I begged the Lord three times to take this problem away from me. **9** But he said to me, My grace is enough for you. When you are weak, my power is made perfect in you*
2 Cor 12 : 8 (NCV)

Paul had a "Thorn in the Flesh" just like many other believers. His writings tell us that there was something in his life that discouraged, hurt or distressed him. Remember, Paul was as human as we are and he became discouraged with his thorn to the point that three times he asked the Lord to take it away, but the Lord had other ideas! Have you ever experienced that?

No one knows for sure what Paul's thorn in the flesh was. Circumstances, bad eyesight, depression, some kind of recurring temptation? I really don't know, but I have a personal feeling it might just have been Paul's memories of persecuting, arresting and imprisoning believers or worse! It is just possible that these memories may have haunted him in his Christian ministry and had the effect of keeping him humble.

So, the most important thing for us to notice today is not Paul's thorn, or even the personal thorns we might be struggling with. It is God's reply to Paul's earnest prayer for release because it was in effect "no" but the Lord added,

My grace is enough for you. When you are weak, my power is made perfect in you."

So often people struggle with the thorns of memories, guilt, pain, disappointment or perhaps persecution, and these things can hold us back. When this happens, we overlook the truth that the Lord revealed to Paul. The amazing truth is that with every thorn, trial or pain comes grace!

In the Lord's response to Paul's prayer it is as if the Lord was saying, "Paul, My power is more than a match for whatever you are facing. By my Grace you, in your weakness, can turn to me, and through your simple faith my Grace (unmerited mercy and favour) opens the way for Me to make you strong"

Put simply, as we lean on the Lord and give Him our burdens, His grace and His strength flow into and around us. So rather than coping with the thorn ourselves His strength gives us the victory.

Do you have a thorn today? The Psalmist said,

> *Cast your burden on the LORD, and he will sustain you; he will never permit the righteous to be shaken.* Psalm 55:22 NIV

So yes, thorns can indeed be a blessing when we approach them as Paul was encouraged to approach his because, with the pain of a thorn can come strength and blessing, but only when we surrender the thorn to allow His grace to open the way for us to be given the victory of heaven.

Prayer.

Lord thank you for your unbounded grace,
forgive me when I think more about the thorns
in my life and neglect you. Help me to lean
heavily on you through the grace you have
given me through my Lord Jesus. Amen

Day 55

Shamgar

It's amazing how the Bible highlights giants of the faith in verses we often overlook. Shamgar is one such person, he was the third Judge in Israel and killed 600 Philistines with an ox goad, thus saving Israel. Although he did great exploits we know very little about him.

> *After Ehud, Shamgar son of Anath rescued Israel. He once killed 600 Philistines with an ox goad.* Judges 3:31 NLT

After his death Debora the only woman judge in Israel sang about him,

> *"In the days of Shamgar son of Anath, and in the days Jael, people avoided the main roads, and travellers stayed on winding pathways.* Judges 5:6 NLT

Shamgar's father's name was Anath, which is a name referring to a Canaanite deity, so some people assume Shamgar was the son of a mixed Israelite-Canaanite marriage which of course was forbidden by the Lord.

So Shamgar could be said to be an example of God working through a person with a dubious background because of his heart. The Lord used this one man with a piece of wood to rescue His own people from the Philistines and thus changed many lives for the good.

We don't know very much more about Shamgar.

However, this principle still stands today. God will use anyone who makes themselves available to Him regardless of their past. We are each called to live for God and when we do that our actions really do have a tremendous influence on people.

I remember how one day a tradesman was working in our house and in chatting, he asked me where I was from. I said that originally, I came from Essex and then explained how I had been a pastor prior to my retirement and had moved around the country in different churches. His immediate response was "I knew it! There is something about you" I asked him, what makes you say that? he replied and I quote, "I really don't know, you are just nice and there is something about you!" The truth is that when we sincerely live for the Lord, unbeknown to us people can be strangely touched by something they find indefinable but real. That's Jesus in us.

God wants to use people like us to bless and touch who knows how many lives? In all probability our Godly influences on folks may never be seen by us, but that does not matter. Is very possible that the Lord wants to use you like He did Shamgar, either in a dramatic or quiet way to be a force for good in someone's life. Background is unimportant because it's our heart right now that matters.

Prayer,
        Father help me to have a heart like Shamgar willing to be used by you whenever you wish. Lord bless other people through me I pray. Amen

Day 56

Walking Alone

Pay careful attention to your own work, for then you will get the satisfaction of a job well done, and you won't need to compare yourself to anyone else." Gal 6:4 NLT

In the western church we come under the influence of Bible teachers who rightly emphasise the importance of ongoing relationships with other believers. So, in addition to church attendance, personal growth groups, mentoring a host of other support things are available to us. Today's reading does not concern itself with properly qualified and structured counselling, rather generic fellowship groups found in many churches. In this context supportive fellowship can be very good but can also become a problem if taken out of a biblical context.

You see interdependency is good if it is teamwork involving mutual love and support, this is because these things can foster growth in a positive way. However, it can also become a problem if we are predisposed to being easily affected by external circumstances, such as other people's opinions of us and their shared concepts of what is good for us. When this happens, we can innocently fall into the trap of being falsely influenced in our spiritual well-being. Interdependence like this can then become negative.

It is a basic biblical principle that we all come into the world naked and leave in much the same way! In this life it's only our personal relationship with God that stands us in good stead for eternity. No support group or mentor will stand with us to support or advise us when the time comes to depart from this life, only the good shepherd of our souls. So, this is where the rubber hits the road in the Christian life and is really at the heart of our text. An important question then for all of us is "how well do we walk with God when in isolation?" It's on this basis that we will give an account one day!

Our text today says "Pay careful attention to your own work" this means not relying on others for our daily walk or perceived worth. Friends and mentoring groups are fine but nothing can ever replace the personal work of getting to know and trust Jesus more each day. Spend time with Him alone, talk naturally to Him and ask Him to talk back to you. Listen to that still small voice in your heart and daily build up your personal relationship with Him. In this way you are paying attention to your own work and you will never have to measure yourself against any other person.

Prayer

> Jesus, please help me to listen to your voice and to walk closer to you each day, building only on my relationship with you. Thank you for all my friends and supporters, bless them but never let them take your place Lord. Amen

It Really Matters What We Believe.

Over the next three days we are going to look at the subject of our Lord's Resurrection.

> *On the first day of the week, very early in the morning, the women took the spices they had prepared and went to the tomb. 2 They found the stone rolled away from the tomb, 3 but when they entered, they did not find the body of the Lord Jesus. 4 While they were wondering about this, suddenly two men in clothes that gleamed like lightning stood beside them. 5 In their fright the women bowed down with their faces to the ground, but the men said to them, "Why do you look for the living among the dead?* Luke 24:1-5 (NIV)

The most important question a person can ever ask in this life is "Did Jesus really rise from the dead? This is because if He did then obviously heaven, forgiveness and eternal life are a reality and Jesus demonstrated that when He came out of the grave.

However, if He did not rise from the dead then His own promises were blatantly untrue and the early church was guilty of deliberately misleading people. The apostle Paul put it very bluntly when he said if there was no resurrection then we are unchanged and still in our sin.

And if Christ has not been raised, our preaching is useless and so is your faith. 15 More than that, we are then found to be false witnesses about God, for we have testified about God that he raised Christ from the dead. But he did not raise him if in fact the dead are not raised.16 For if the dead are not raised, then Christ has not been raised either. 17 And if Christ has not been raised, your faith is futile; you are still in your sins
1Cor 15 14 (NIV)

It was reported in 2017 that a quarter of British people who described themselves as Christian said they did not believe in a literal Resurrection, so there is a problem somewhere! If we don't accept the bodily resurrection of Jesus then we reduce Christianity to the level of other world religions, all of which have dead founders. This in turn opens the door to concluding "all roads lead to God" Which is obviously the very opposite to what Jesus said,

Jesus answered, "I am the way and the truth and the life. No one comes to the Father except through me" John 14:6 (NIV)

However, scripture is its own best interpreter and illuminator, far superior to any logical human argument so let's notice what Paul had previously said,

For what I received I passed on to you as of first importance: that Christ died for our sins according to the Scriptures, 4 that he was buried, that he was raised on the third day according to the Scriptures, 5 and that he appeared to Cephas, and then to the Twelve. 6 After that, he appeared to more than five hundred of the brothers and sisters at the same time, most of whom are still living, though some have fallen asleep. 7 Then he appeared to James, then to all the apostles, 8 and last of all he appeared to me also, as to one abnormally born 1 Cor 15:3-7 (NIV)

According to Paul's words immediately after the Resurrection a minimum of 500+ people testified to physically seeing the risen Jesus. I am not aware of history recording any who later said, "I'm sorry I was mistaken!" Then, there was massive growth in the early church. This growth was through people who experienced Jesus resurrection power in their conversions, and remember this phenomenal growth continues to this very day!

Why not take a moment to look into your heart and ask, "Do I really believe Jesus rose from the dead, or does it all seem too fanciful to be true?" Tomorrow we will look at the problems we will have if we don't accept Jesus rose from the dead. Then on the third day we will see the benefits of believing in the resurrection

Prayer

Jesus, I believe you rose from the dead and came out of the grave literally, thank you for dying for me, thank you for rising for me and thank you for accepting me. Amen

(www.bbc.co.uk/news/uk-england-39153121)

It Matters What We Believe.

On the first day of the week, very early in the morning, the women took the spices they had prepared and went to the tomb. 2 They found the stone rolled away from the tomb, 3 but when they entered, they did not find the body of the Lord Jesus. 4 While they were wondering about this, suddenly two men in clothes that gleamed like lightning stood beside them. 5 In their fright the women bowed down with their faces to the ground, but the men said to them, "Why do you look for the living among the dead? Luke 24:1-5 (NIV)

Yesterday we began to look at the importance of believing in a literal Resurrection of Jesus because it really does matter what we believe in matters of biblical doctrine. The Nicene Creed states that "On the third day, he rose again" That line is pivotal. It declares that three days after Jesus died on the cross, he was resurrected; this gave a glimpse of eternal life for all believers. The core and heart of Christianity is a risen saviour, no resurrection means a dead Jesus!

So today we are going to think of the difficulties we have if we don't accept the resurrection. As we said yesterday, in April 2017 it was reported that a quarter of people who consider themselves Christian do not believe in the resurrection.

Some people interpret the resurrection story as symbolism. For them the Easter story simply illustrates that new life comes around regularly, much like daffodils or snowdrops after a long winter. Sadly though, reducing the resurrection in this way leaves people with nothing at the end of their lives, only vagueness and the uncertainty of unbelief.

Human life only has logical meaning when we accept that the creator God has applied intelligent design in His creation and therefore is working to an eternal plan. In the Christian worldview, the resurrected Jesus is the bedrock of the Father's eternal plans and purposes. Without the resurrection human life has no meaning and we are all reduced to being products of random chance and evolution, doomed to nothingness when we die. Doubting the literal resurrection leaves us with nothing concrete to believe in. But the actual resurrection which is so verifiable has created a seismic shift from that position. This is why Christians are like Abraham looking for the eternal city.

> *By faith Abraham, when called to go to a place he would later receive as his inheritance, obeyed and went, even though he did not know where he was going. 9 By faith he made his home in the promised land like a stranger in a foreign country; he lived in tents, as did Isaac and Jacob, who were heirs with him of the same promise. 10 For he was looking forward to the city with foundations, whose architect and builder is God.*
> Heb 11:8 (NIV)

Again, if Jesus did not rise from the dead then Christianity must be a lie and delusion. This is because so much about Jesus and the Resurrection is written in biblical promises, prophecies, eye witness accounts and of course Jesus own words. These all add to the overwhelming weight of evidence for the resurrection, but if Jesus is not resurrected then all the evidence crumbles bringing into disrepute the whole bible.

I know today's reading is solemn but it's vital that we know where we stand on the resurrection. It really does matter because our faith stands or falls on this truth.

Prayer

> Jesus without you and your glorious resurrection I am lost, help be to stand firm on all the Bible teaches about your glorious resurrection. Amen

It Matters What We Believe

On the first day of the week, very early in the morning, the women took the spices they had prepared and went to the tomb. 2 They found the stone rolled away from the tomb, 3 but when they entered, they did not find the body of the Lord Jesus. 4 While they were wondering about this, suddenly two men in clothes that gleamed like lightning stood beside them. 5 In their fright the women bowed down with their faces to the ground, but the men said to them, "Why do you look for the living among the dead? Luke 24:1-5 (NIV)

Over the past two days we have been considering the resurrection of Jesus. We have seen the positive fact of the resurrection and the negative effects of not accepting it. Today we are going to see the benefits of accepting this amazing truth.

The Lord Jesus's resurrection is the Father's heavenly guarantee that all Christian believers will be resurrected at Christ's second coming. Jesus demonstrated resurrection power when the Godhead raised Him from the grave after three days, utterly victorious over death and the devil!

Salvation is only found in a personal relationship with Jesus and this is only possible because of the resurrection. This was the Father's divine plan for our redemption, a Living Saviour,

> *Therefore, he is able to save completely those who come to God through him, because he always lives to intercede for them.*
> Heb 7:25 (NIV)

Accepting the truth of the resurrection in our hearts brings the witness of the Holy Spirit that right now, this very moment, Jesus having ascended into heaven is praying for us. He is continually showing His wounds thus declaring our total forgiveness by the shedding of His blood on Calvary. The following brief points underline a few of the glorious effects of the literal resurrection for us as believers.

Only a risen saviour can forgive sins,

> *To him all the prophets bear witness that everyone who believes in him receives forgiveness of sins through his name.*
> Acts 10:43 *(ESV)*

Through Jesus rising from the dead we experience justification; thus, we have clean hands and hearts before God,

> *He was delivered over to death for our sins and was raised to life for our justification.*
> Romans 4:25 (NIV)

The rising of Jesus demonstrates that He will never again taste death,

> *For we know that since Christ was raised from the dead, he cannot die again; death no longer has mastery over him*
> Rom 6:9 (NIV)

One day we will be raised just like Him.

> *But Christ has indeed been raised from the dead, the first fruits of those who have fallen asleep* 1 Cor 15:20 (NIV)

My friend, the resurrection of Jesus is not symbolic, it's not a fable, it is the most stupendous thing that has happened since creation. Jesus is alive, do you believe that? Can you walk in that glorious truth with the witness of the Holy Spirit in your heart?

The Nicene Creed says. For our sake he was crucified under Pontius Pilate; he suffered death and was buried. On the third day he rose again in accordance with the Scriptures; he ascended into heaven and is seated at the right hand of the Father. He will come again in glory to judge the living and the dead, and his kingdom will have no end....."

Remember it matters what we believe, if you have doubts about the resurrection just ask Jesus to reveal Himself to you, do that in sincerity and you won't go far wrong!

Prayer

Lord Jesus I praise you because you are alive right now, I believe in your resurrection, you tasted death in order that I might taste eternal life. From the bottom of my heart, thank you Jesus!

Day 60

Peace in Generosity

Good will come to those who are generous and lend freely, who conduct their affairs with justice. Surely the righteous will never be shaken; they will be remembered forever. 7 They will have no fear of bad news; their hearts are steadfast, trusting in the Lord. 8 Their hearts are secure, they will have no fear
Psalm 112:7 (NIV)

Our text today should really be read in the light of the whole Psalm so if you have time, look at the full ten verses.

It's a sad fact of life that at times 99.9 percent of the news on TV is negative. However, we don't have to live in fear of evil things, because of our relationship with Him. Of course, this doesn't mean that we are always exempt from bad news or dangerous situations, but it does mean that we don't have to live in anxiety and fear because,

The eternal God is your refuge, and underneath are the everlasting arms
Deut 33:27 (NKJ)

Our text today shows us that if we live in the right way, God honours us and provides strength and provision for each day. There are keys however to experiencing this blessing found in our text,

Good will come to those who are generous and lend freely!

We need to look into our hearts and ask "Am I generous with my time for others and generous with my financial giving"? Rather than just being governed by what I think is convenient or affordable.

My wife and I have personally proved more times than we can remember that God honours a generous spirit, whether it is money, time or something else. This equally applies to individuals, churches and ministries. I remember once our church leadership deciding to give away the very small amount of church money we had in the bank, leaving it empty! The day we planted that seed in generosity our church finances began to be utterly revolutionized and have been so ever since.

A generous person will prosper; whoever refreshes others will be refreshed. Pro 11:25

Of course, generosity is only one aspect of right living, but in our materialistic world it is often the most neglected. However, if we pay attention to this one simple truth then our reward is as our text says,

Surely the righteous will never be shaken; they will be remembered forever. 7 They will have no fear of bad news; their hearts are steadfast, trusting in the Lord. 8 Their hearts are secure, they will have no fear;

Yes, we live in days of tribulation and trouble but because we are in relationship with our creator through Jesus we can enjoy the benefits of obedience.

I wonder if this kind of reading blesses or annoys you? because I have touched on giving. Just remember God owns everything we have, He loans it to us for this life then it goes to someone else. He expects our lives to mirror Him and His generosity in the way we deal with others, remember this includes money, time, kindness and a host of other areas in our lives.

Prayer,

Father, teach me to be generous in my dealings with you and those about me. Forgive any meanness on my part and help me to mirror to the world your great generosity and love. In Jesus Name Amen.

Day 61

God's Torn Curtain

And when Jesus had cried out again in a loud voice, He gave up his spirit. At that moment the curtain of the temple was torn in two from top to bottom Mat 27:50-51(NIV)

Did you ever try to walk into a shop and end up confronted with a "No Entry sign"? The door would only open towards you because it was intended as an exit for people on the other side! Embarrassing but hardly the end of the world!

In the Old Testament this is exactly what confronted people who tried to approach God. No Entry! So, someone had to stand in the gap for them because without the High Priest and the offerings it was hopeless. Form the earliest times God had been remote in this sense from His chosen people. He is Holy and we are not and that was an impenetrable barrier between God and man. Job lamented this fact but that's for another day.

In Jesus time the Temple in Jerusalem had a veil some 4 inches thick that separated the Holy of Holies from the people. The book of Exodus tells us that this thick veil was fashioned from blue, purple and scarlet material, combined with linen. This was God's barrier and only the high priest could enter but then only once a year.

At the moment that Jesus died on the cross a number of unnatural and incredible things took place,

> Earthquake, Matt. 27:51
> Dead raised Matt. 27:52
> Darkness Matt. 27:45
> Temple Veil Torn Matt. 27:51

However, today we are specifically thinking about the torn veil. So, what is the significance of this strange event? Notice, it was torn from heaven i.e. from top to the bottom. Only God could do that because of its height. The tearing of the veil at the moment of Jesus' death dramatically demonstrated that His sacrifice and shedding of His blood, was the sufficient atonement for all our sins. The way to God was now open and through the death of Jesus, Jews as well as Gentiles could now approach God! At the tearing of the veil, God moved away from the temple, never again to dwell in a building made by human hands.

> *"The God who made the world and everything in it is the Lord of heaven and earth and does not live in temples built by human hands Acts 17:24* (NIV)

The temple had served its purpose and the whole religious system of approaching God was now finished. The temple and Jerusalem would now be destroyed by the Romans in A.D. 70, just as Jesus prophesied,

> *Jesus left the temple and was walking away when his disciples came up to him to call his attention to its buildings.2 "Do you see all these things?" he asked. "Truly I tell you, not one stone here will be left on another; everyone will be thrown down."*
> Matt 24:1 (NIV)

The Temple and the veil had proved the continuation of the old covenant dating from Moses time and earlier but now Jesus had established the New Covenant in His blood! We identify with this every time we take communion.

> *This is my blood of the covenant, which is poured out for many for the forgiveness of sins.* Matt 26:28 (NIV)

Today let's be thankful for all that Jesus has done for us, we have free access through His blood and there is no sin that the Father won't forgive through Jesus when we come in repentance and seek forgiveness.

Are you hiding something and keeping it back from His grace? We do that to our own hurt because we have access through the New Covenant in Jesus blood.

Prayer,

> Thank you, Father, that there is no curtain dividing us today, thank you Jesus because you have opened a New and Living way for me to enjoy forgiveness and peace with my heavenly Father. Amen

Day 62

Regrets

Simon, Simon, Satan has asked to sift all of you as wheat.32 But I have prayed for you, Simon, that your faith may not fail. And when you have turned back, strengthen your brothers."33 But he replied, "Lord, I am ready to go with you to prison and to death." 34 Jesus answered, "I tell you, Peter, before the rooster crows today, you will deny three times that you know me....................
Luke 22:31-34 (NIV)

..........."The Lord turned and looked straight at Peter. Then Peter remembered the word the Lord had spoken to him: "Before the rooster crows today, you will disown me three times.
Luke 22:61 (NIV)

I am sure we are all familiar with this story of Peter. In the closing hours of our Lord's earthly life, Peter made a rushed and ill thought out statement to the effect that he would never, under any circumstances, leave Jesus, even to the point of death. However, a very short time later, he openly and angrily denied that he knew Jesus and with an oath! (Matt 26:72) just because of his personal fear of what might happen to him!

Think with me for a few moments about these words *"The Lord turned and looked straight at Peter."* Can you imagine how Peter felt as the Lord turned and looked at him? He must have been overwhelmed with guilt as well as full of fear over what he had done and probably very angry at himself, because after all he had publicly denied that he even knew Jesus let alone loved him! His personal life had taken a crash and his situation was a total disaster.

The fact that Jesus looked at him and his immediate reaction reveals a lot about Peter and even more about Jesus. Peter had just learned a lesson, no matter how determined he was or how strong he thought he was, he was made of dust! I don't think Peter was really a coward but he was human, capable of failing without even trying! Yet his reaction when he saw Jesus look at him was one of instant regret,

>*He went outside and wept bitterly.*
>Luke 22:62 (NIV)

Although he failed, his reaction showed that his heart had been touched and realising his sin he was full of remorse. The only way that he could express that inner feeling was to cry bitterly. We too are human and prone to fail but when we realise our sin we too should be full of remorse because that leads to repentance.

>*Godly sorrow brings repentance that leads to salvation and leaves no regret, but worldly sorrow brings death.* 2 Cor 7:10

We also learn something about Jesus from this story. *The Lord turned and looked straight at Peter.* How did Jesus look at him? Was it an accusing look, a look of anger, surprise, disappointment or disapproval? No! Jesus looked at him with love in His eyes and total acceptance, not rejection. Think of this for a moment, the Lord turned away from His physical suffering to look at Peter! How He loved him.

We need to learn from this story, the Lord does not reject us when we fail but He looks with love and acceptance, as long as our reaction is right when we realise we have failed. Judas failed and he took a different course of action but that is another story to be told.

Are you struggling with a failure of some sort? Feeling perhaps things have gone too far? Be encouraged that the Lord Jesus still looks on you with love and acceptance in His eyes, just make sure you do your part and react in the right way.

Prayer,

> Lord Jesus I have failed you so many times and I am sorry, please restore me the way you restored Peter who went on to be used by you in amazing ways. Use me Lord for your glory. Amen

Day 63

Encouragement

Then Samuel took a stone and set it up between Mizpah and Shen. He named it Ebenezer, saying, "Thus far the LORD has helped us." 1 Sam 7:12 (NIV)

Do you ever feel like you just need someone to come alongside and encourage you? I do, and I guess everyone feels this to one extent or another depending on their makeup and circumstances. Our text today originated when God had thundered against Israel's enemies and routed them. At this point the Prophet Samuel made an offering to the Lord and said these words *"Thus far"*

If you are feeling low today or in need of spiritual support do what Samuel did, cast your mind back and remember just how good the Lord has been in your life. You may not feel very blessed at this moment in fact you may feel quite low, but I wonder how your life would be without the Lord's care and protection in all your yesterdays? I dread to think where I might be!

So today endeavour to remember, as His child the Lord is always with you, the Holy Spirit always hovers around you and Jesus always walks beside you. Jesus said,

I will not leave you as orphans; I will come to you. John 14:18 (NIV)

Yes, we all need to be encouraged at times and the encouragement of fellow believers is important but can't begin to compare to the encouragement the Lord gives by the Holy Spirit when despite feeling low we reach out in faith to Him. I read this today, "God is with you and His timing is perfect". Perhaps that's for someone reading this book just now.

So, try to do what King David did when he was under pressure,

> *And David was greatly distressed; for the people spoke of stoning him, because the soul of all the people was grieved, every man for his sons and for his daughters: but David encouraged himself in the LORD his God.*
> 1 Sam 30:6 (NKJV)

So, your encouragement will spring from faith and hope in our eternal Lord and saviour Jesus. Lift your heart to Him once again today and encourage yourself in the Lord and walk in the footsteps of Samuel and King David.

Prayer.

> Lord when I feel low and discouraged, please draw near to me, let me feel your love and power again. Like Samuel I want to say in faith, "Thus far the LORD has helped me". Help me to walk always in this reality. Amen

Day 64

What is God's Will for Me?

He has shown you, O mortal, what is good. And what does the Lord require of you? To act justly and to love mercy and to walk humbly with your God. Micah 6:8 (NIV)

Perhaps you spend time asking "What is your will for me Lord" either for today or indeed for the rest of my life?

So, let me share with you one of the lessons I have learnt in my life. So many times, in my early life as a Christian I asked this question in relation to my personal future. I felt called to Christian service but that was it! I was unsure which way to move forward. I pushed on many doors and to be honest had a few hard kickbacks. If I had known then what I am going to share with you now things would have been much easier for me!

Knowing God's will in our lives comes from the way we approach things. First of all, note the key words of our text, *"what does the Lord require of you? To act justly and to love mercy and to walk humbly with your God"*

Whatever situation we are in, or questions we may have about our lives, these words are the secret of us moving forward.

Everything in the Christian life is born out of our relationship with the Father through Jesus and no matter who we are or what our situation, revelation is born out of these two things.

Firstly, the words *"To act justly and to love mercy"* addresses our personal integrity with the Lord and our fellow man. We cannot allow ourselves to entertain any lack of integrity in our dealings with the Lord nor indeed with our fellow man. It matters what we think, watch and dwell on in our innermost hearts and how we deal with people.

The second is *"to walk humbly with your God"* True humility is in very short supply these days, so many see it as a weakness both outside the church and sadly within the body of Christ. Pride, self will and other manifestations of the flesh all go directly against God's revealed will for His children. God Himself will not bless the human heart if it goes against His revealed word.

If we are longing to know God's will for our lives then we must attend to these two points because revelation of the sort we are looking for flows out of relationship which in turn naturally flows out of a correct walk with the Lord.

Don't try to rush like I did, just walk correctly with God and relax in Him. He always works to His time table, He leaves nothing to chance and is never early or late in His leading or answers to prayer for that matter.

Prayer,

Lord, as I seek to walk in a way pleasing to you, help me to have the grace to put right things that stop me hearing your voice. Lord, my heart is yours take me and lead me according to your perfect will. Amen.

A Different Spirit

> *But because my servant Caleb has a different spirit and follows me wholeheartedly, I will bring him into the land he went to, and his descendants will inherit it.*
> Num 14:24. (NIV)

The Lord looks for people who have the willingness to have a different spirit within themselves. Of course, this willingness is aided by the Holy Spirit who, through Jesus, is changing us from one level of glory to another. As Paul said,

> *And we all, who with unveiled faces contemplate the Lord's glory, are being transformed into his image with ever-increasing glory, which comes from the Lord, who is the Spirit.* 2 Cor 3:18 (NET)

Having a different spirit impacts our everyday walk, but what does a different spirit look like? Well for example, a person with a different spirit does not major on criticising others. They look for ways to commend and lift up others,

> *Finally, brethren, whatsoever things are true, whatsoever things are honest, whatsoever things are just, whatsoever things are pure,*

whatsoever things are lovely, whatsoever things are of good report; if there be any virtue, and if there be any praise, think on these things" Phil 4:8 (NKJ)

A person with a different spirit is a thankful person. Thankful to the Lord for whatever today may bring along. Not everything that happens to us is good and that is where our faith comes in, because a different spirit encourages us to look upward in every situation.

A person with a different spirit rests in God for their needs and knows He never fails us nor will He forget us as Jesus said

"Therefore, I tell you, do not worry about your life, what you will eat or drink; or about your body, what you will wear. Is not life more than food, and the body more than clothes? [26] Look at the birds of the air; they do not sow or reap or store away in barns, and yet your heavenly Father feeds them. Are you not much more valuable than they? [27] Can any one of you by worrying add a single hour to your life[a]?and why do you worry about clothes? See how the flowers of the field grow. They do not labour or spin. [29] Yet I tell you that not even Solomon in all his splendour was dressed like one of these. [30] If that is how God clothes the grass of the field, which is here today and tomorrow is thrown into the fire, will he not much more clothe you—you of little faith? [31] So do not worry,

*saying, 'What shall we eat?' or 'What shall we drink?' or 'What shall we wear?'*³² *For the pagans run after all these things, and your heavenly Father knows that you need them.*³³ *But seek first his kingdom and his righteousness, and all these things will be given to you as well.* Matt 6:25-33

It takes a conscious act of our will to seek to have a different spirit, it's no good passively sitting in the midst of our circumstances and waiting for our spirit to just change, we have to actively seek to move up a gear in a spiritual sense.

As you approach this unknown day be encouraged to seek a different spirit and keep looking upwards whatever happens.

Prayer

> Heavenly Father, thank you for today. Holy Spirit, help me to be different and a person who trusts you more today than I did yesterday.